Utah Women and the Law

Financial support for the second revised edition
was generously provided by AT&T

Utah Women and the Law
A Resource Handbook

Governor's Commission for Women and Families

Second Revised Edition

University of Utah Press
Salt Lake City

∞ The paper in this book meets the standards for permanence and durability established by the Committee on Production Guidelines for Book Longevity for the Council on Library Resources.

Library of Congress Cataloging-in-Publication Data

Utah women and the law : a resource handbook / Governor's Commission for Women and Families. — 2nd rev. ed.
p. cm.
Includes bibliographical references.
ISBN 0-87480-365-9)(prbk. : alk. paper)
1. Women—Legal status, laws, etc.—Utah. I. Utah. Governor's Commission for Women and Families.
KFU91.W6A87 1991
346.79201'34—dc20 90-43194
[347.9206134] CIP

C

CONTENTS

C

C

P

PREFACE

Utah Women and the Law: A Resource Handbook is a project of the Utah Governor's Commission for Women and Families (formerly the Commission on the Status of Women). Its purpose is to provide an overview of the laws that deal with the most common problems faced by women and to suggest agencies to contact and questions to ask. This handbook is intended to be a practical guide on basic legal matters, but by no means should it be considered a substitute for competent legal counsel.

The first edition was published in 1987. The handbook was written by legal experts who contributed their time and expertise along with members of the Governor's Commission. The services contributed for the development, publication, funding, and distribution of this document have been remarkable and essential. If you have suggestions for future editions of the handbook, please call the Commission office at 538-1736.

Utah Women and the Law: A Resource Handbook is dedicated to the women of Utah. The inspiration for its publication came from an awareness of the courage and determination of Utah women to live meaningful lives and actively to seek better conditions and circumstances for themselves and others.

ACKNOWLEDGMENTS

A project such as this reflects the professional expertise and personal compassion of literally dozens of people who have felt the need of Utah's women for a better understanding of how they relate to the legal system. We gratefully recognize the hundreds of hours volunteered to complete *Utah Women and the Law: A Resource Handbook.*

We acknowledge again with appreciation the original authors, whose contributions were recognized in the first edition of this handbook:

Jaynne Allison
Brian M. Bernard
Gayle Brice
Mimi S. Buescher
Kaye M. Coleman
Kathryn Collard
Jane Reister Conard
Michael Dazey
Brenda L. Flanders
Barbara B. Hales
Karen Suzuki-Hashimoto
Chizuko Ishimatsu
Karen Knight-Eagan
Linda Stengel Lepreau
Anne Milne
Barbara W. Richman
Jan L. Tyler
Sue Ann Walker
Paul M. Warner

We also thank those who have participated in the updating and revision of the text for this second edition. The Revision Committee was co-chaired by Grethe B. Peterson and Patricia S. Drawe, and its members included Pat Christensen, Cecelia Espenoza, Brenda Flanders, and Karlynn Hinman.

Contributors to this edition of the handbook include Patricia S. Drawe, managing attorney, Mountain Fuel Supply Company (''Consumer Rights and Responsibilities''); M. Karlynn Hinman, Kirton, McConkie & Poelman (''Employment'' and ''Physical and Mental Health''); Colleen Larkin Bell, staff attorney, Questar Corporation (''Children'' and ''Housing and Landlord/Tenant Relations''); Brenda L. Flanders, attorney at law (''Property Rights and the Making of a Will''); Martha M. Pierce, Utah Legal Services (''Utah Marriage and Divorce Law''); Ward Harper and Mary J. Kienitz, Utah Legal Services (''Social Welfare Laws''); Margaret M. Frank, senior attorney, Questar Corporation (''Taxes''); Barbara W. Richman, Standing Chapter 13 and 12 Trustee (''Money Problems and Bankruptcy''); Jo Carol Nesset-Sale, Haley & Stoleburger (''Jury Duty and Voting Rights''); Glen A. Cook, Lt. Commander, JAGC, U.S.N.R. (''Women and the Military''); Cecelia M. Espenoza, Deputy Salt Lake City Prosecutor (''Small Claims Court'' and ''Criminal Law'').

We also acknowledge the Young Lawyers section of the Utah State Bar Needs of the Elderly Committee for its preparation of Utah Senior Citizens Handbook, portions of which have been incorporated into this volume.

Those providing technical assistance also merit our warm appreciation: Susan Robinson, Connie Driggs, and Vicky Lopez for typing, editing, and preparing the manuscript.

Sincere thanks also to the former and present members of what is now the Utah Governor's Commission for Women and Families and to Governor Norman Bangerter, who encouraged and supported the creation and updating of this handbook.

Kathleen C. Mason, Chair
Utah Governor's Commission for
Women and Families
June 1990

GOVERNOR'S COMMISSION FOR WOMEN AND FAMILIES COMMISSIONERS 1989–1990

Dolores B. Bennett
Vee Carlisle
Patricia S. Drawe, Esq.
Barbara B. Hales
Shirley R. Johnsen
Kathleen C. Mason, Chair
Noemi P. Mattis, Ph.D.
Bonnie Miller
Beth D. Quist
Pauline Richards
Dolores M. Riley
Marianne Stoddard
Olene S. Walker, Ph.D.
Representative Beverly J. White
Margaret D. Wilson
Colleen Colton, Ph.D.
(Governor's Liason to the Commission)

Commission Telephone Number
(801) 538-1736

1

CONSUMER RIGHTS AND RESPONSIBILITIES

SECTION A: CONSUMER CONTRACTS

As a general rule, once you have signed a contract you are responsible for doing what the contract requires.

If you cosign with another person such as your spouse or child, you will be responsible for making payments if the other signer defaults, unless you are released by the creditor. Even if you are divorced and your spouse is ordered to pay family debts, the creditor can still hold you responsible under the terms of the contract. Before you sign any contract, inform yourself about all the terms of the contract and ask questions about anything you don't understand. Be sure you understand common contract terms. For instance, you should know the type of contract you are signing.

Retail installment contract: Sometimes referred to as a conditional sales contract, this allows you to receive merchandise at the time of signing. If you fail to fulfill the contract, the seller can demand immediate payment or repossess the merchandise.

Promissory note: This is a signed agreement between you and a cash lender. If the stated terms of repayment are not met, the lender can get a court judgment against you.

What happens if you don't pay:

Repossession: If you stop making payments on goods you have, the lender can pick up the goods and sell them to satisfy the loan agreement. The seller also has the option of taking you to court instead of repossessing the goods.

Court order to garnishee wages: The creditor may get a court order that requires your repayment. The court has the power to direct your employer to pay the creditor an amount of up to 25 percent of your weekly disposable income.

The creditor may file a lawsuit: If you do not keep your part of the agreement, you can be sued by the creditor. If you have good cause for not paying, such as the goods not being received, you must present this evidence in a court of law.

There are some contract clauses to beware of:

Acceleration clause: This allows the creditor to demand immediate and full payment of the unpaid balance if you miss one or more payments. If the contract is for merchandise, the creditor can repossess the item and you are still liable for the unpaid balance.

Add-on clause: This allows you to buy additional merchandise and have the financing added on to your original contract. It has the appearance of giving you liberal credit privileges, but the catch is that it also allows the seller to repossess all the merchandise if you fail to complete payment on the add-on item.

Attorney's fees clause: If your creditor must repossess an item or sues you to collect payment, this clause requires you to pay for all legal fees incurred by the creditor.

Balloon clause: A contract with this kind of clause has a final payment that is much larger than the preceding payments. If you fail to make this last payment, you may be forced to refinance at a higher rate of interest or have your merchandise repossessed.

Lien against your property: If you don't pay an obligation secured by a lien, the creditor can seize *anything* of value you own and sell it to satisfy the debt.

Wage assignment: This clause allows a creditor to collect a certain percentage of your wages from your employer should your payments become overdue. This is not the same as wage garnishment, which can occur only as a result of a court order.

Other contract provisions: Hidden costs lurk in the shadows of virtually every major sale. Be sure you know whether you must pay extra for delivery. Is there a service contract connected with the product that you don't really need? If you are purchasing on credit, do you understand all of the credit terms, including the finance charge? Do you wish to purchase credit insurance? How much does credit insurance add to the total cost? Know the answers before you sign any agreement. Remember the general rule—once you have signed, you are responsible for doing what the contract requires.

SECTION B: PRODUCT WARRANTIES

A warranty is a promise made by the seller or manufacturer guaranteeing the quality and performance of an item. Typically a warranty will explain what the seller or manufacturer will do for you if the item is defective. It is always a good idea to ask about the warranties that may accompany an item you are thinking about buying. If a salesperson states that a product has a guarantee or warranty, you should ask for a written copy of it. Beware of promises made orally by a salesperson, like "this is the best deal in town," or "this engine has another 100,000 miles of life in it." You should be particularly alert for the words "as is" (typically in used-car sales) which may appear on a sales contract. If you buy an "as is" product, the seller makes no promises about its quality or performance.

SECTION C: CONSUMER CREDIT

CONSUMER CREDIT RIGHTS

Under the Fair Credit Reporting Act and Equal Credit Opportunity Act you have a number of rights that are summarized as follows:

You have the right to—

Receive credit in your own name if you meet the creditor's standards.

1 Use a cosigner who is someone other than your husband, if one is needed.

Refuse to answer questions about your plans for having or raising children.

Keep your own accounts after marriage, divorce, or widowhood as long as you meet the creditor's criteria.

Have public assistance, alimony, pension, and child support considered as any other income.

Know the specific reason your application for credit was turned down.

Present information to the creditor which shows that your husband's credit rating, if it is bad, doesn't reflect your willingness or ability to pay.

Demand that any incorrect information in your file be changed.

Have your side of the story placed in the credit bureau file if unfavorable information cannot be eliminated.

DISCLOSING COSTS OF CREDIT

To clarify the cost of borrowing money, the Utah Consumer Credit Code (UCCC) requires a lender to make certain written "disclosures" to a potential borrower. A consumer is entitled to receive these disclosures before the credit transaction is completed. Unfortunately, in many instances these disclosures only confuse consumers. Because of this, you should ask questions before you borrow. Make sure you understand the written disclosures, their effect, and interest rates. Know how much it actually costs you to borrow money.

INTEREST RATES

The maximum rate of interest that generally can be charged to a consumer is 21 percent. If a creditor charges more than this rate, the creditor may be guilty of "usury." The penalties for usury may include a refund of interest payments, a fine, or imprisonment of the creditor. However, there is no limit on the interest rate that may be charged on a revolving credit card account. Make sure you understand how much interest you are paying on credit card purchases, and shop around for the best interest rates.

LATE CHARGE FEE

Creditors base interest-rate charges on the assumption that you will make your payments on time. If you fail to make a payment as scheduled, the creditor may impose a one-time late payment penalty fee of $15 or 5 percent of the late payment, whichever is greater. Late charges are not part of the finance charge, but the penalty fee must be disclosed to you before you enter the credit transaction.

RIGHT TO A REBATE WHEN LOAN IS PREPAID

If you pay off a loan before repayment is due, you are entitled to a partial refund of the interest you paid in advance. Before you enter a credit transaction, a lender must tell you the method by which a refund will be calculated.

RIGHT TO CANCEL

You are guaranteed the right to cancel a consumer credit transaction without any penalty (1) if you put up your home to secure repayment of your loan or (2) if the sale of goods on credit was solicited and completed at your home or place of employment. If you decide to cancel such a credit transaction, you must notify the creditor within three business days after completing the transaction. The creditor must return any deposit or money you paid and cancel the security agreement within ten days after receiving your notice. You must then return any goods you received as a part of the transaction. This right to cancel is often referred to as a "cooling-off period," but a seller does not need to let you out of a deal just because you have second thoughts. Except as described above, a seller is entitled to enforce the terms of a contract once you have signed it.

SECURITY INTEREST

To ensure repayment of money you borrow, a lender may require that you pledge some of your property as collateral. This means that you agree that the creditor may take the pledged property from you if you fail to repay your loan. This arrangement is called a security interest.

COURT JUDGMENT

If someone obtains a court judgment against you, it is important to know how the judgment can be collected. Once a judgment has been obtained against you, and is entered into the district court records, it becomes a lien against all real estate owned by you in the county where it is recorded. The person with the judgment against you may be able to force the sheriff to sell your house and collect the amount of the judgment from the sale proceeds.

The person with a judgment against you may also take personal property away from you. However, a number of items are exempt from collection. They include clothing, household furniture, household utensils and appliances, and similar personal property that is "reasonably necessary for one household"; the house or mobile home in which you live, to the value of $8,000 for the head of the family and additional amounts for a spouse and dependents; tools, machines, furniture, books or other property used in your trade or business valued at less than $500; certain life insurance money; public assistance; an interest up to $1,500 in one motor vehicle; and other assets traceable to certain awards and rights. These exceptions do not apply if you have voluntarily given the creditor a lien on your property. Social Security and VA benefits and other retirement income cannot be taken from you except for payment of federal taxes, child support, or alimony.

If you have a judgment against you, be sure to seek advice from an attorney to be certain your rights are protected.

CREDIT CARDS

When you apply for a credit card, the company issuing the card must tell you when it will charge interest and finance charges, how high its interest will be, and the minimum payments required. Each billing statement you receive will tell you how the finance charge is determined, how long you can postpone paying without having to pay a finance charge, and the minimum payment required.

Your billing statements must contain an address to which you can write if you disagree with your bill. If you disagree with your bill, you must write to your creditor within sixty days from the date of the statement and tell the creditor why you believe your bill is wrong. The creditor must respond to your disagreement about the bill within thirty days and resolve the dispute within two billing cycles, but not more than ninety days. So long as the dispute is not resolved, you do not need to make any payments for the amounts in dispute. The creditor may not collect any disputed amounts or any finance charges on those amounts.

Until a creditor carries out these error resolution procedures, he cannot close your account, nor can he adversely report on your credit standing because of your failure to pay the disputed amounts. If a creditor does not follow these procedures, he must forfeit the disputed amount, up to $50, regardless of whether an error was made.

Utah law protects you from illegal use of your credit cards. You are liable for a maximum of $50 in losses in the case of unauthorized use of any credit card that has been stolen from you, if you report the theft to your credit card company.

WHAT TO DO IF YOU ARE DENIED CREDIT

If you are denied credit, you must be told why. Your denial of credit may be based upon a credit bureau report—a report prepared by a company that specializes in keeping files on the credit history of people who borrow money and repay loans. When a credit bureau report is the reason you are denied credit, you can ask about the information contained in your credit file and request an investigation to determine if that information is complete and accurate. If the credit bureau made an error in compiling your credit-history file, it must correct the error. If your dispute with the credit bureau is not resolved, you can submit a written statement to the credit bureau reporting your side of the story. Your statement will become part of your permanent credit record. In addition, if you believe there is inaccurate or misleading information in your credit-history file that is not corrected, you can complain to the Federal Trade Commission or the Credit Division of the Utah Department of Financial Institutions.

CREDIT INSURANCE

Credit insurance is a type of insurance that is sold in connection with loans and credit sales. Credit life insurance will pay off a loan if the borrower dies. Credit accident and disability insurance will make payments if a borrower is sick for an extended period or disabled. Credit insurance, however, is very costly and has questionable value. It is rarely necessary and normally should be avoided. Although it is optional, in most cases borrowers who purchase it are not adequately informed and do not know that they are paying for the insurance.

SECTION D: COMMON TRANSACTIONS AND PROBLEMS

REPAIR AND ESTIMATE FRAUD

In Utah, consumers are entitled to a written estimate of charges for repairs that exceed $25. Unfortunately, a merchant or mechanic does not need to volunteer the estimate. Instead, you must request it. Once you obtain a written estimate, you must authorize any additional charges that exceed 10 percent of the original estimate.

AUTOMOBILE REPAIRS

When you are confronted by a repair bill that you are unable or unwilling to pay because the mechanic demands payment for unauthorized or defective work, you may get possession of your car by posting a bond with the circuit court. The mechanic may then sue to collect the amount of the bill, but you have the use of your car in the meantime. Bonds may be purchased from most insurance agents. The clerk of the local circuit court will provide you with the necessary forms to take advantage of this law.

Also, Utah has a "lemon law," which provides you with an effective remedy if you have purchased a new car that is defective. The law requires the manufacturer or its authorized dealer, within one year of your purchase, to make all repairs promised in the express warranty that came with your new car. The manufacturer may have to replace your new car (1) if the same defect has been subject to repair four or more times during one year, or (2) if your car is out of service for thirty or more business days during your first year of ownership. If you think you may be entitled to have your defective car replaced, contact the Utah Division of Consumer Protection.

UTILITY PROBLEMS

If you have problems with a public utility, call the company involved and ask to speak to a special consumer representative or call the Utah Division of Public Utilities at 530-6652. The Public Service Commission has issued rules governing utility service to residential customers; a summary of these rules is to be provided to customers at least once a year.

DOOR-TO-DOOR SALES (See ''Right to Cancel,'' above.)

TELEPHONE SALES

You may become legally bound to purchase goods or services as a result of a telephone conversation. Of course, making purchases over the telephone can be risky business; it does not lend itself to prudent comparison shopping. If you are interested in the goods or services offered through telephone solicitation, you should obtain the name and telephone number of the caller and follow up the call with your own call to the Division of Consumer Protection, Utah Department of Commerce, or the Better Business Bureau. If a telephone seller is reluctant to give you the information that you request and pressures you to make an immediate purchase, beware and hang up.

SECTION E: RESOLVING CONSUMER DISPUTES

CONSUMER COMPLAINTS

Most business people give the benefit of the doubt to customers who have complaints. For this reason, you should always take your complaints to the seller first. When you do, provide the seller with copies of all important documents, such as bills, receipts, cancelled checks, and repair estimates. Be calm and persistent. If your complaints are not satisfied, contact the manufacturer of the product or the head office of the store (if it is a chain). Once again, explain your problem as simply as possible and include copies of documents. If you still get nowhere, you must look for outside help.

When you have an unresolved problem with a business, you can submit a written complaint to the Division of Consumer Protection, Department of Commerce (530-6601). The division evaluates your written complaint, and if it feels the complaint is valid, it contacts the business in an attempt to work out a solution. If your problem is with an out-of-state mail order company, the division contacts the out-of-state seller or asks the attorney general of the seller's home state to investigate the matter and intervene on your behalf. If the division determines that a lawsuit is necessary to resolve the problem, it will refer your case to the Utah Attorney General. You can also resolve consumer disputes through small claims court, if necessary. (See chapter 16.)

ATTORNEYS

When self-help fails, you may want to seek the assistance of an attorney. If you have a low income, you may contact an office of Utah Legal Services. The Utah State Bar Association will provide you with the names of attorneys who will discuss your problem with you for one-half hour at a nominal cost.

CLOUT WITH YOUR CREDIT CARD

Finally, if you have a VISA or Mastercard or other credit card, you may find it useful in helping you to resolve consumer disputes. You have added protection if you are dissatisfied with a product or service costing more than $50 that you purchased by credit card within 100 miles of your home. (Mail and telephone purchases made from your home are treated as though they were made within 100 miles.) To obtain this added protection, you should first make an effort to resolve the problem with the seller. If you are unsuccessful, you should notify your credit card company, and it will remove the charge for the items in dispute until your problem is resolved. However, before taking this step, you should make sure that your complaint is legitimate, because the seller reserves the right to sue you in court to recover the purchase price.

COLLECTION TACTICS

Collection agencies and credit departments often use forceful and questionable methods to collect debts. They may try to embarrass you at your place of employment or in your neighborhood. They may threaten to do things they cannot legally do. ("If you don't bring me $50 by Friday, I will have the sheriff pick up your car.") They may also try to make a person without assets pay even though they know the person cannot be legally forced to pay.

Reasonable collection practices are legal. However, if the agency makes unreasonable threats, uses harassment to an extreme, or engages in libel or slander, it breaks the law. In such cases, consult an attorney or complain to the Division of Consumer Protection.

2

2 EMPLOYMENT

WOMEN IN THE WORK FORCE AND DISCRIMINATION LAW

There is a growing awareness that women play a legitimate and significant role in today's work force. Economic demands and personal goals lead many women to consider careers rather than merely jobs. One barrier to full employment of women will be removed when discrimination is completely eliminated.

Working women currently earn only about two-thirds of what working men make. Although federal and state laws require equal pay for equal work and although great strides have been made by women employees in many occupations, many women still face disparate treatment and disparate opportunities to engage in higher paying employment.

Many laws and executive orders prohibit employment discrimination on the basis of race, religion, national origin, age, and gender. These laws are complicated and often confusing, but they offer genuine help in combating gender discrimination. Each major law governing employment is different. Laws vary in the range and types of employers covered, the types of discrimination prohibited, their scope of protection, the methods of enforcement, the procedures which must be followed, and the time limits on complaints.

If you believe you have been subjected to discrimination or unfair treatment, you should assert your rights under the applicable laws as quickly as possible. Since you must comply with the requirements of each law under which you may have a claim, it is wise to consult both the Utah Anti-Discrimination Division of the State Industrial Commission (UADD) and a lawyer to obtain help with employment discrimination claims.

CAN I BE FIRED AT ANY TIME?

For a number of years, Utah has been an "employment-at-will" state, which means that an employer could terminate an employee "at will" or at any time unless the employee had a written contract or unless the employee could prove that the employer had violated a law by terminating unjustly, for example, because of unlawful discrimination.

The Utah Supreme Court has recently modified the employment-at-will doctrine, making it possible for an employee, in some circumstances, to defend against an at-will termination. The law is complex, so it is wise to consult with an attorney if you have been fired.

If you were employed for a probationary or fixed period or to perform a specific task, you can be legally terminated at the end of the probation, at the end of the specified period, or whenever the task is done. Be sure that you understand fully the terms of the probation, time limits, or other conditions in an employment agreement.

WHAT FEDERAL LAWS ADDRESS JOB DISCRIMINATION?

1. *Title VII of the Civil Rights Act of 1964, as amended* (Title VII), is the most comprehensive employment discrimination law prohibiting employment discrimination on the basis of race, color, religion, sex, or national origin. It prohibits virtually all forms of discrimination by private employers with fifteen or more employees; employment agencies; federal, state, and local governments; public and private educational institutions; and labor unions, including labor-management

committees for apprenticeship and training. Title VII forbids practices which are intentionally discriminatory as well as those which have a discriminatory effect.

Title VII recognizes limited exemptions, permitting religious employers to prefer their own members for jobs in nonprofit activities, and allowing discrimination by employers when an otherwise prohibited classification is a bona fide occupational qualification. For example, a film maker can hire a white, male actor to play George Washington.

Title VII created the Equal Employment Opportunity Commission (EEOC), which administers and enforces the act. A complaint under Title VII must be filed with the EEOC or a state human rights agency before it can be taken to court.

2. *The Equal Pay Act of 1963* (EPA) provides that equal pay must be given for substantially equal work performed by women and men in the same company or government office. "Equal work" considers tasks requiring equal skill, effort, responsibility, or training. Tasks should be substantially similar but need not be identical. For example, the pay for a female bookkeeper can be compared to that of a male bookkeeper working on a different ledger, but not to that of a male clerk.

The EPA does not apply to pay differences unrelated to sex. For example, it is legal to pay more according to seniority, merit, or productivity.

The EPA covers most private employees and federal, state, and local government employees, including executive, administrative, and professional employees in companies engaged in commerce. "Commerce" has been interpreted broadly to cover nearly all employers.

The EPA is administered by the EEOC, but, unlike a Title VII claim, you may file an EPA suit directly in court.

3. *The Age Discrimination in Employment Act of 1967* (ADEA) prohibits age discrimination against individuals between the ages of forty and seventy, but if you have a federal job there is no maximum age.

The ADEA applies to employers of twenty or more persons,

employment agencies, labor unions with more than twenty-five members, and public employers. It prohibits age discrimination in hiring, firing, training, promotion, compensation, or in other terms, conditions, or privileges of employment.

For example, an employer may not discharge an older, more expensive employee to hire a younger worker who will cost the company less in salary and benefits. However, the ADEA does not prohibit discrimination based on *necessary* job qualifications or standards of per formance. Thus, an employee aged sixty-five can be fired if unable to do the job.

The EEOC administers and enforces the ADEA. Claims should be filed with the EEOC.

4. *The Rehabilitation Act of 1973* prohibits discrimination in employment on the basis of physical or mental handicap.

''Handicap'' means a physical or mental impairment that substantially limits one or more life activities, such as caring for oneself, walking, seeing, or hearing. ''Mental impairment'' means any psychological disorder or condition, physical impairment, cosmetic disfigurement, or anatomical loss, including mental retardation or other related mental impairment.

Employers must provide ''reasonable accommodation'' to the handicaps of otherwise qualified workers with known physical or mental limitations unless accommodation would impose ''undue hardship'' on the business. ''Accommodation'' may include, but is not limited to, access (like restroom stalls large enough for wheelchairs), restructuring jobs to allow part-time or modified work schedules, acquiring or modifying equipment, adjusting or modifying examinations (for instance, reading questions to a blind applicant), and providing services such as interpretation for the deaf.

Contact the EEOC for information regarding filing claims under this law.

5. *Executive Order 11246*, as amended by Order Number 11375, and Executive Order 11478 prohibit discrimination on the basis of race, color, religion, sex, or national origin in federal offices or in companies which have contracts with the federal government.

In general, businesses with contracts over $50,000 and fifty or more employees must take affirmative action, that is, establish goals and timetables for full and equal employment opportunities. The exact scope of required affirmative action in government contracting and other employment has been the subject of several major court challenges. If you think affirmative action may be relevant to your particular job or a job application, consult with the Labor Department, Office of Federal Contract Compliance Program, Federal Building, 125 South State, Salt Lake City, Utah 84147, (801) 524-4470. The Office can tell you the dollar amounts per contractor that are needed to qualify and should be able to assist you with other relevant information.

6. *The Fair Labor Standards Act of 1938* (FLSA) provides fair labor standards for private companies involved in or providing services in interstate commerce, some retail and service establishments, and federal, state, and local governments. The exceptions include schools, hospitals, fire prevention, police protection, public health, parks, and recreation.

FLSA establishes minimum wage, overtime pay, record keeping, and child labor standards for full-time and part-time workers. Covered employees must be paid for all hours worked in a work week—the time an employee must be on duty or at the prescribed place of work. Overtime pay must be at least one and one-half times the employee's regular pay rate for each hour worked.

In Utah, call the Wage-Hour Division, U.S. Department of Labor, Federal Building, 125 South State Street, Salt Lake City, Utah 84147, (801) 524-5706.

If you make a complaint, FLSA-authorized representatives will investigate, gathering data about employment conditions or practices to determine compliance. If violations are found, the investigators may recommend changes in employment practices. Willful violations may be prosecuted criminally with fines, and a second conviction may result in imprisonment. Violators of child labor provisions are subject to a civil penalty for each violation. It is also a violation to fire or harass an employee for filing a complaint.

WHAT UTAH LAWS ADDRESS JOB DISCRIMINATION?

1. The *Utah State Fair Employment Practices Act,* also called the *Utah*

Anti-Discrimination Act, prohibits discrimination in employment because of race, creed, color, sex, religion, ancestry, national origin, handicap, and age if the individual is forty or older.

2. The *Governor's Code of Fair Practices,* Executive Order of May 4, 1979, prohibits discrimination in employment because of race, color, sex, religion, national origin, age, or handicap by all state agencies and state contractors, including state licensing and regulatory agencies and by private employers with at least twenty-five employees.

3. The Governor's Executive Order of December 6, 1973, created the Office of Equal Employment Opportunity Program and requires state agencies to have Affirmative Action Plans (AAP).

Utah law varies only slightly from federal law. The UADA prohibits discrimination based on race, religion, color, sex, age, ancestry, national origin, and handicap for employees or applicants for jobs where there are twenty-five or more employees. The act excludes religious organizations, associations or corporations, or any other corporation or association that is owned by a religious organization, association or corporation, or a bona fide private membership club (other than a labor organization).

WHAT DO THE LAWS COVER?

Title VII prohibits discrimination in classified advertisements that list a job preference (for example, "job opportunities—women") and forbids discriminatory testing for new applicants or for promotions. All testing must measure job performance.

Title VII prohibits discriminatory recruitment, hiring, and firing. For example, an employer cannot fire a woman because she "didn't fit in" with male employees. Title VII prohibits discriminatory compensation, assignment, classification, transfer, promotion, layoff, or recall. An employer cannot pay different salaries because one worker is male and another female. Company facilities and training and apprenticeship programs must be equally available.

Title VII forbids discrimination in fringe benefits, such as life and health insurance, retirement plans, and disability leave, except with respect to pregnancy, which is discussed later. Title VII also protects employees who use the procedures described in EEO legislation from employer retaliation.

Recently the United States Supreme Court has considered so-called "mixed motive" cases in which a woman has been bypassed for promotion or other job-related benefit because of a mixture of illegal discrimination and legal considerations about her skills and performance and the employer's needs. A majority of the Court has held that, if the woman can show that an illegal reason led to an adverse employment decision, the employer then has the burden to show that the adverse decision would have been made on legitimate factors and without the illegitimate or discriminatory one.

IS "SEX" EVER A LEGAL JOB REQUIREMENT?

Identifying a particular gender for a job is lawful in the few instances when only a man or only a woman can do it, when sex is a bona fide occupational qualification (BFOQ) for that job, e.g., actor (male) or actress (female). Very few jobs can be done only by men or by women. An employer cannot advertise for "salesmen" only. Anyone with the required experience may apply. Similarly, women generally cannot be excluded from jobs because of dangerous conditions when it is no more dangerous for a woman than for a man.

WHAT ARE DISCRIMINATORY QUESTIONS IN A JOB INTERVIEW?

The EEOC regulations do not list questions that are expressly prohibited or improper. EEOC states that it looks with "extreme disfavor" on inquiries about race, color, religion, or national origin unless it is a BFOQ. The employer must show that the qualifications are reasonably necessary for the performance of the particular job.

Even if men and women are asked the same questions—for example, "Are you married?" "Do you have children?"—the questions may be discriminatory because the answers have different implications for women. Utah's Anti-Discrimination Act does not specifically list improper questions, but questions designed to elicit information about race, creed, sex, color, ancestry, or national origin are improper. For instance, requests for photographs (which would reveal race) should be made only after hiring.

WHAT IS SEXUAL HARASSMENT?

The EEOC defines sexual harassment as "unwelcome sexual advances, requests for sexual favors, and other verbal or physical conduct of a sexual nature." Both men and women can commit sexual harassment. If the boss occasionally calls you "honey" or invites you out, even if you do not like the language or the invitation, these actions may not constitute sexual harassment in the legal sense. For you to have a legal claim, harassment must be related to a job or job conditions. For example, if a promotion is conditioned upon sexual favors, the condition is harassment. If you have refused to be involved in sexual conduct and any adverse decision about your job is related to your refusal, the adverse decision indicates harassment. Sexual talk or action is harassment when it "unreasonably interferes" with work performance or creates an intimidating, hostile, or offensive working environment. In some situations, an employer must control sexually offensive statements or actions by one employee directed against another or be liable for harassment against the offended person.

Consult with the EEOC or an attorney to determine whether your situation or problem may give you legal recourse.

CAN I BE DENIED A PROMOTION OR FIRED BECAUSE I AM PREGNANT?

The Pregnancy Discrimination Act, a 1978 amendment to Title VII, provides that women affected by pregnancy and related conditions must be treated the same as other applicants and employees on the basis of their actual ability or inability to work.

You cannot be fired or refused a job or promotion merely because you are pregnant or have had an abortion. You cannot be forced to take maternity leave if you can still work. You cannot be prevented from returning to work after maternity leave if other employees entitled to disability leave are entitled to get their jobs back. You cannot be denied disability benefits or sick leave if other employees who are unable to work for medical reasons get benefits or leave.

An employer may establish time requirements and may prove business necessity to deny return employment in some cases. The burden of proof rests with the employer to prove the business necessity.

Some states require that, in general, a woman be returned to the same or a comparable position upon return from pregnancy. Utah has not extended its law that far, but new laws or regulations are being considered at both state and federal levels. If you are or wish to become pregnant, ask your employer about company policy. You may also wish to consult with the EEOC, a lawyer, or a counseling agency to determine what rights you will have and what job security or reemploy-
2 ment you can expect.

CAN AN EMPLOYER MAKE DECISIONS BECAUSE OF SEXUAL PREFERENCE?

None of the many bills that have been introduced in Congress to outlaw discrimination against homosexuals have passed. Title VII's ban on sex discrimination is directed toward gender, not sexual practices or preferences.[1] Some municipalities have adopted ordinances prohibiting employment discrimination against lesbians and homosexuals, but no such prohibition is in effect in Utah at present.

WHAT ABOUT RELIGIOUS DISCRIMINATION?

An employer must "reasonably accommodate" your religious beliefs, practices, or observances when they conflict with your job-related duties. However, an employer need not make accommodations that would impose an "undue hardship" or burden to the business. For the purposes of Title VII, religious belief is a broad concept that encompasses sincerely held ethical and moral beliefs as well as traditional religious views and affiliations.

Religious employers may prefer their own members for employment in their nonprofit activities, even though religious membership or status may not be required by the job itself.

WHAT DOES "NATIONAL ORIGIN" MEAN?

The EEOC defines "national origin" discrimination broadly as including, but not limited to, the denial of equal employment opportunity because of personal or ancestral origin or because of the physical, cultural, or linguistic characteristics of a national group. EEOC considers height and weight requirements suspect if they tend to exclude individuals on the basis of national origin and are not clearly related to the needs of a particular job.

WHEN MUST I FILE A COMPLAINT?

You must file a complaint under the Utah Anti-Discrimination Act or under the Acts which the EEOC administers within 180 days of the event or occurrence. The Utah Anti-Discrimination Division of the State Industrial Commission (UADD) can accept a complaint for the EEOC under a work-sharing arrangement between agencies. In certain circumstances you may have up to 360 days to file a claim, but in order to protect your rights, especially if you are uncertain whether you should file under state or federal law or both, act promptly and file your complaint promptly with the UADD.

If you are a federal employee or are employed by a contractor with a government contract, you have thirty days in which to contact the agency's Equal Employment Opportunity counselor. Twenty-one days after your final interview with the counselor, you will receive notification of the steps necessary to pursue your complaint if it has not yet been resolved. You then have fifteen days in which to make a formal written complaint.

If your job problem involves the FLSA (a wages and hours complaint, for example), make your complaint with the Wages and Hours office of the Labor Department.

An attorney can assist you in filing and making a complaint, but only if you act promptly.

HOW AND WHERE CAN I FILE A COMPLAINT?

In Utah, any person who is an employee or potential employee where twenty-five or more are employed (fifteen in federal offices) may file a complaint of discrimination because of race, color, sex, age, religion, ancestry, national origin, or handicap with the Utah Anti-Discrimination Division, Utah Industrial Commission, 160 East 300 South, Salt Lake City, Utah 84110-5800, (801) 530-6801 or see listing under "Utah State Government," "Industrial Commission" of Utah. The office also accepts complaints from groups.

You may make complaints in person or in writing, but not by telephone.

WHAT IF I WORK FOR THE GOVERNMENT?

If you are a federal employee or are employed by a federal contractor, you must file with the agency involved, meeting the time limits specified. The agency will hold an investigation and, based on the investigative record, make a recommendation. If you disagree with the recommendation, you are given a limited number of days to file a request for a hearing with the EEOC, which will conduct a fact-finding hearing and an investigation to determine probable cause.

WHAT DO I NEED TO FILE A COMPLAINT?

Complaint forms ask for your name, address, and telephone number; the name and address of the alleged violator, your description of the problem or objectionable practice, and the harm you have suffered.

You should provide clear information about the parties and the problem and should have in mind the remedy you are seeking. Do you want to be rehired? Do you want only back pay? Awards for back wages are limited to two years prior to the date on which you filed your complaint.

Your records will be kept confidential, but the employer will be notified of your charges.

WHAT DO I HAVE TO DO TO PROVE DISCRIMINATION?

Employment discrimination cases use two general concepts to identify unfair treatment:

1. *Disparate treatment:* the employer treats some people less favorably than others because of their race, color, religion, sex, national origin, or age—for example, if women are not considered for promotions to managerial levels.

2. *Disparate impact:* the employer's practices look neutral but, in reality, fall more harshly on one group than another and cannot be justified by business necessity.

WHAT HAPPENS AFTER I FILE MY CHARGE WITH UADD?

Your employer receives a copy and is asked to respond within ten days. After UADD receives the response, it holds a fact-finding conference with you and your employer. If you cannot settle at that point, UADD appoints an investigator to collect more information. After investigation, the UADD investigator drafts a determination of cause or no cause, meaning there is cause for complaint or no cause.

HOW DO I BRING SUIT?

You must file any suit within certain time limits. In the case of age discrimination, you must wait thirty days before you can file. You must file Title VII complaints within 180 days after you have made your written complaint. The Industrial Commission allows thirty days after the final decision is made on the complaint.

Consult either UADD or EEOC and seek legal counsel to protect your rights and to meet time requirements.

WHAT IF THE BOSS RETALIATES?

Reprisals and harassment of the employee are unlawful. You can file a second charge of retaliation against a harassing employer or employees. The employer will then be notified of the second charge.

WHAT SHOULD I DO IF MY UNION HAS DISCRIMINATED?

If you are represented by a labor union that has fifteen or more members, you are probably protected against union discrimination by UADA and by Title VII. You can follow the same procedures as against employers, and you can also seek redress under the procedures of the National Labor Relations Act, which considers discrimination by a union to be an unfair labor practice.

3

3

EDUCATION

WHAT ARE THE LEGAL RIGHTS OF WOMEN IN THE AREA OF EDUCATION?

Traditionally, education has been a recognized and effective way for individuals to change their economic and social circumstances. Just as education can be the key to improving the quality of life, barriers to education can lock doors, preventing educational and economic opportunities. Therefore, equal access to and opportunity in education is a critical issue for Utah women.

Often those seeking to change existing prejudices and customs have met with hostility and ridicule. Many of the legal, social, political, and economic rights women enjoy and accept so naturally today were won by early-day and modern pioneers, sometimes at great personal cost.

Until recently, sex discrimination in education was largely ignored, unchallenged, and unchecked. Indeed, such discrimination against women in the educational community was not illegal.

The Ninety-Second Congress enacted a national policy that placed in motion the mechanism to end discrimination. The Equal Pay Act of 1963, effective in 1964, amended the Fair Labor Standards Act to require that men and women performing equal work must receive equal pay. Title VII of the Civil Rights Act of 1964 was amended in 1972 to prohibit discrimination on the basis of sex in all administrative, executive, and professional employment practices in education, as well as in employment. In the same year Title IX of the Education Amendments of 1972 passed, prohibiting sex discrimination against students and employees in federally assisted educational programs. Subsequently, other interpretive guidelines have been issued which make sexual harassment illegal under Title VII of the Civil Rights Act of 1964 and Title IX of the Education Amendments of 1972 as amended. Another important source of help to women experiencing job discrimination in education because of sex is not a law passed by Congress, but rather Executive Order 11246, issued by the President of the United States. Forbidding discrimination against minorities in employment, it was signed by President Lyndon B. Johnson in 1965, amended by Executive Order 11375 effective in 1968 to include a ban on discrimination because of sex.

Other legislation has been enacted to protect women from discrimination in employment, in education, and in access to educational programs and activities. These include the Age Discrimination Act, Pregnancy Discrimination Act, and Sections 503 and 504 of the Rehabilitation Act of 1973.

WHAT IS SEX DISCRIMINATION?

Sex discrimination is any action that denies a person opportunities, privileges, roles, or rewards on the basis of his or her sex.

HOW CAN I RECOGNIZE SEX DISCRIMINATION?

Look for instances in which women or men are treated differently just because of their sex, and you will see how they are hurt by such treatment.

As a check, ask yourself a couple of questions:

Am I being treated differently from students/teachers of the opposite sex?

Am I experiencing any barriers due to differential treatment on the basis of sex?

If your answer to either question is yes, you have most likely encountered some form of sex bias or discrimination.

WHAT IS TITLE VII?

Title VII of the Civil Rights Act, as we have said, prohibits discrimination in employment including education on the basis of race, color, religion, national origin, or sex. All institutions or agencies with fifteen or more employees, including state and local governments and labor organizations, are covered under the amended act. Title VII prohibits discriminatory practices in all terms and conditions of employment including the following:

Recruitment, selection, assignment, transfer, layoff, discharge, and recall

Opportunities for promotion

In-service training or development opportunities

Wages and salaries

Sick leave time and sick pay

Vacation time and vacation pay

Overtime work and overtime pay

Medical, hospital, life, and accident insurance

Retirement plans and benefits

Other staff benefits

The enforcement agency is the Equal Employment Opportunity Commission.

WHAT IS EXECUTIVE ORDER 11246?

Executive Order 11246 addresses nondiscrimination under federal contract in two major areas:

Affirmative action must be taken to ensure that students and/or applicants are employed and are treated after employment without regard for race, creed, color, religion, national origin, sex, or age. Affirmative action further requires that the employer make additional efforts to recruit, employ, and promote qualified members of minority groups formerly excluded. 3

Nondiscrimination requires the elimination of all prohibited discriminatory conditions.

Under Executive Order 11246 discrimination in employment is prohibited in—

Employment, upgrading, demotion, or transfer

Recruitment or recruitment advertising

Layoffs or termination

Rates of pay or other forms of compensation

Selection for training, including apprenticeship

Unless positive action is taken to overcome the effects of systematic forms of discrimination, federal funds can be denied.

The Office of Federal Contract Compliance (OFCCP) enforces this order.

WHAT IS TITLE IX OF THE EDUCATION AMENDMENTS OF 1972?

Title IX of the Education Amendments of 1972 is a federal law designed to eliminate discrimination in educational programs and activities on the basis of sex. All institutions receiving federal funds are required to comply with the law in the admission and treatment of their students.

Title IX prohibits discrimination on the basis of sex in—

Admission to vocational, graduate, professional, and public undergraduate schools

Access to courses and programs

Counseling and guidance

3 Tests, materials, and practices

Physical education and athletics

Vocational education programs

Student rules and policies

Financial assistance (including student employment)

Student housing

Extracurricular activities

Employment in educational institutions

Activities of enrolled students, including academic, extracurricular, and research activities

Career development and placement services

Health services

Conditions related to pregnancy (such disabilities are to be treated the same as any other temporary disability)

The enforcement agency of these amendments is the Office for Civil Rights/Equal Opportunity or the agency funding the project.

WHAT IS THE EQUAL PAY ACT OF 1963?

The Equal Pay Act prohibits unequal pay for men and women who work in the same establishment and on jobs requiring equal skill, effort, and responsibility which are performed under the same working conditions.

The Equal Pay Act prohibits discrimination on the basis of sex in—

Wages and fringe benefits

Sick leave and vacation leave

Health and life insurance

Pensions

Credit union benefits

Other retirement benefits based on sex

The Equal Employment Opportunity Commission enforces this act.

WHAT IS AGE DISCRIMINATION?

The Age Discrimination Act of 1967 (employment) and the Age Discrimination Act of 1975 (programs or activities) as amended, are designed to prohibit discrimination on the basis of age in employment and in programs or activities receiving federal financial assistance. Any employment decision relative to a person between the ages of forty and seventy must be based on the individual's ability or capacity to perform the work in question. The Equal Employment Opportunity Commission enforces these acts.

WHAT IS TITLE VI OF THE CIVIL RIGHTS ACT OF 1964?

Title VI of the Civil Rights Act of 1964 provides that no person in the United States will, on the grounds of race, color, or national origin, be excluded from participation in, be denied the benefits of, or be subjected to discrimination under, any program or activity receiving federal financial assistance.

Responsibility for enforcement of Title VI rests with the Department of Education (formerly HEW), which has the power to withhold federal funds from any educational institution that practices discrimination based on race, color, or national origin.

Title VI prohibits discrimination on the basis of race, color, or national origin. It is illegal to—

Deny any individual any service, financial aid, or other benefit that is provided in a different manner from that provided to other individuals under the program.

Subject an individual to segregation or separate treatment in any matter related to his or her receipt of any service, financial aid, or other benefit under the program.

Restrict an individual in any way in the enjoyment of any advantage or privilege enjoyed by others receiving any service, financial aid, or other benefit under the program.

Treat an individual differently from others in determining whether he or she satisfied any admission, enrollment, quota, eligibility, membership, or other requirement or condition which individuals must meet to receive any service, financial aid, or other benefit provided under the program.

Deny a person the opportunity to participate as a member of a planning or advisory body that is an integral part of the program.

HOW DOES TITLE VI AFFECT MINORITY WOMEN?

Sections 503 and 504 of the Rehabilitation Act of 1973 are designed to eliminate discrimination on the basis of handicap in any program, including education, receiving federal financial assistance.

An institution may not, in providing any employment, aid, benefit, or service on the basis of handicap—

Deny a qualified handicapped person employment or the opportunity to participate in or benefit from any aid, benefit, or service.

Offer a qualified handicapped person employment or an opportunity to participate in or benefit from any aid, benefit, or service that is not equal to that afforded others.

Provide a qualified handicapped person with an aid, benefit, or service that is not as effective as that provided to others.

Perpetuate discrimination against a qualified handicapped person by providing significant assistance to an agency, organization, or person that discriminates on the basis of handicap in providing any employment, aid, benefit, or service to beneficiaries of any program.

Deny a qualified handicapped person the opportunity to participate as a member of planning or advisory boards.

Limit a qualified handicapped person in his or her employment or in the enjoyment of any right, privilege, advantage, or opportunity enjoyed by others receiving an aid, benefit, or service.

WHAT IS THE DEFINITION OF "HANDICAPPED"?

Section 504 of the Rehabilitation Act of 1973 defines as *handicapped* "any person who (1) has a physical or mental impairment which substantially limits one or more of such person's major life activities, (2) has a record of such an impairment, or (3) is regarded as having such an impairment."

Under this definition, *handicapped* can encompass any individual who is confined to a wheelchair, blind, alcoholic or formerly alcoholic, addicted or formerly addicted to drugs, epileptic, diabetic, mentally impaired, or directly affected or limited in his or her major life activities, whether or not the condition is hidden.

Accessibility is a major part of Section 504. All handicapped individuals should have access to all programs and/or buildings, classrooms, and facilities on the campus. At present, every effort is being made to make all buildings and facilities accessible to all individuals. The Equal Opportunity Office should be notified of any area or program on campus that is not accessible to everyone.

The Office of Federal Contract Compliance enforces Section 503, and the OFCCP and the OCR/EO enforce program equality.

BEFORE I FILE A COMPLAINT, WHAT DO I NEED TO CONSIDER?

If you feel that you have been discriminated against, you should—

Try to resolve the complaint informally at the lowest level, i.e., supervisor, teacher, principal, etc., or discuss the concern with the grievance officer or a knowledgeable person.

Request that your conversation or inquiry be kept confidential.

Provide receipts, contracts, or other records supporting your claim of discrimination.

Identify witnesses who have information regarding your claim.

Determine what you want to have happen to remedy the claim, i.e., back pay, promotion, transfer, grade change, access to programs and activities, etc.

If you decide to file a complaint alleging discrimination, it is important to look carefully at the risks and trade-offs that are part of such a decision. By filing a complaint, you run the risk of alienating those you file the claim against and others in the system. Although the grievance procedure should be viewed as a means to resolve problems in a fair and equitable manner, it is often perceived as a confrontational course of action. Be prepared for the emotional cost often inherent in pursuing such a course of action.

HOW DO I FILE A COMPLAINT?

In any grievance or complaint, it is important to start with those processes available to you within the institution. When those options have been exhausted, you can move to external remedies.

You are responsible for documenting the discrimination that happened to you. As soon as you feel you are experiencing discrimination (even if you are not sure), begin to keep a record of what takes place. Include such information as day, complete date, time, place, names of those present, what exactly was said and by whom, what actions took place (verbal or physical threats), names of people who have experienced similar discrimination, copies of correspondence, or any other pertinent documents.

If time has passed and you have not been documenting what has been going on, start immediately to reconstruct what has happened. Include everything you can that is related to your case. Do not personally censor what you deem to be important. Only someone specifically trained can make that determination. Something you feel is unimportant may be important as documentation to support your complaint.

HOW DO I FILE AN INTERNAL COMPLAINT?

Internal complaints refer to complaints filed within the institution where the alleged discrimination occurred. The following procedures should be followed when filing an internal complaint:

Determine the appropriate office or individual to obtain information from regarding the internal grievance and/or appeals process within the institution.

Take action according to the institutional policies.

HOW DO I FILE AN EXTERNAL COMPLAINT?

External complaints refer to complaints filed with the appropriate federal and/or state agency against an institution for alleged discrimination. There are specific federal and state agencies responsible for enforcement of the various laws, depending on the basis of the alleged discrimination. If you decide to file a complaint, it must be done within 180 days of the alleged violation.

4

CHILDREN: CHILD CARE, ADOPTION, SUPPORT, PROTECTION, RIGHTS OF MINORS, AND EDUCATION FOR THE HANDICAPPED

CHILD CARE

Utah has the highest percentage of preschool-age children in the country, and two-thirds of working women with young children are either their family's sole wage earner or are supplementing a family income of $15,000 or less. In 1990, the Utah Legislature established an Office of Child Care to address the significant issue of child care. Congress is also considering federal legislation to assist working parents with child-care needs. Call the state child-care office for help in identifying appropriate child-care options and sources of financial assistance. Also, you should become informed about current tax laws that offer tax breaks for child-care expenses.

ADOPTION

HOW CAN I FIND OUT IF I CAN ADOPT A BABY?

In Utah, any minor child (i.e., a person under the age of eighteen years) may be adopted by any adult person as long as the adopting person is at least ten years older than the adopted child. If a married person wants to adopt a child, his or her spouse must consent to the adoption. If the child is not orphaned, consent to the adoption must be judicially obtained from both biological parents unless they have legally relinquished custody and guardianship of the child (which happens, for instance, when an unwed mother relinquishes a baby for adoption and the father does not claim rights of paternity) or their parental rights have been judicially terminated (as in some child abuse cases). A related situation occurs when the parents have had no contact with the child or have failed to support him or her and the court determines that the child is abandoned. If the parent or parents of a minor child are themselves minors, they are legally treated as adults in regard to their child. For instance, they may validly relinquish their parental rights or consent to an adoption, but if they change their minds later, being minors will not be grounds for revoking the relinquishment.

YOU SAY "PARENTS." WHAT ABOUT GETTING CONSENT FROM THE PUTATIVE FATHER OF A CHILD?

If the baby's biological parents were not married, the father (or man who claims to be the father) may claim rights of paternity by filing a notice with the Department of Health. Forms are available from the registrar of vital statistics or in the offices of any county clerk.[1] The man thus claims (or acknowledges) that he is the child's father and expresses his willingness and intent to support the child to the best of his ability. Once the father has filed this notice, he becomes legally and financially responsible for the child. (He can also be declared the child's father through a paternity suit.) In either case, however, he must claim his rights of paternity before the baby is born but no later than the date the child is relinquished or placed for adoption by the biological mother or the date an adoption petition is filed. If he does not register his claim, he no longer has a legal right to try to establish his paternity, nor will he be able to prevent the child's adoption or relinquishment because, legally, he will be considered to have abandoned the child, waiving any right to notice of proceedings. In cases of "abandonment," the father's consent is not required prior to any adoption or relinquishment.

CAN I ADOPT A BABY IF I'M NOT MARRIED?

Yes. The law states that any adult person (singular) may adopt a child.[2] Thus, a prospective adoption agency cannot deny you a baby simply because you are single. However, since the agency is charged by law to safeguard the child's interests, it may determine—other circumstances being equal—that it is better for a given child to be in a two-parent home. It is best to discuss internal policies frankly with the agency. In any case, the agency will conduct a thorough investigation that includes marital status (married people who have an obviously poor marriage would not be good candidates for adopting a baby), religious background, family constellations, financial position, employment status, personal qualities, and parenting ability.

WHAT ARE THE AGENCIES INVOLVED IN ADOPTION?

4 No person or organization may accept or place for adoption a child who is under the age of eighteen without being licensed by the State Department of Social Services. This department annually reviews every organization, public or private, that is organized as a child placement or adoption agency for fitness and compliance with the department's standards and regulations. Among these requirements are, as a minimum, that the agency or individual will provide a "secure" home for the child, that it will keep and maintain records of the child's vital statistics, and that it will maintain records of the biological and adoptive parents.

The Salt Lake City phone book lists a half-dozen private adoption agencies in its yellow pages, including church-affiliated agencies. All of these must meet the same state requirements. From there, their services may differ. You should contact each agency to determine the length of its waiting list and to get a feeling for how well a particular agency may meet your adoptive needs.

Additionally, if private arrangements are made between parties, the assistance of an attorney is recommended to be sure that the requirements for filing legal documents and making appearances in court are met.[3]

When a private petition for adoption is filed in district court—not through a licensed agency or by a stepparent—the court may order the Division of Family Services to prepare a report within sixty days on the circumstances surrounding the petition: the circumstances of the biological parents, the adoptive parent or parents' financial situation and moral fitness to care for and train the child, the child's physical and mental condition, if it can be determined, and any other factors that may require investigation for the child's welfare.[4] If the report is unfavorable, the court will dismiss the petition and deny the adoption. If the adoption has been processed through a licensed agency, the agency itself will already have conducted the background investigation and determined whether the adoption may proceed.

If you are adopting a child born in another state, either through a private party or through an agency licensed in another state, you must meet specific statutory requirements including providing notice of the intent to adopt to the Division of Family Services. No state, agency, or person may send or receive a child until the state receiving the child sends written notice to the ''sending'' state that it believes the proposed placement is in the child's best interest.[5]

SAY THAT I'M PREGNANT AND CAN'T KEEP THE BABY BUT DON'T WANT AN ABORTION, HOW COULD I PLACE IT FOR ADOPTION?

You can make the arrangements yourself or have an agency arrange to have the child adopted. Typical sources of adoptive parents are through physicians, hospitals, lawyers, licensed adoption agencies, church organizations, or the State Department of Social Services. Licensed agencies and State Social Services may make arrangements for prenatal care, doctor's appointments, medications, hospitalization, delivery costs, and counseling services.

You and the child's father—if he is your husband or has acknowledged paternity—retain full legal right to the child after birth until a permanent relinquishment has been signed by you, the natural parent(s). At the same time the permanent relinquishment is given, a temporary custody order will also be filed and signed by the judge or agency, ordering that the adoptive parents assume the ''custody, care, and control'' of the child pending the final adoption order and decree. This order gives them the legal rights of parents.

The six-months' waiting period is required for the court to be satisfied that the adoption is in the child's best interest and that your consent has been freely given. After the six-months' waiting period, the courts will enter the final adoption order declaring that the child shall henceforth be regarded and treated in all respects as the child of the adoptive parents.[6]

WHAT KINDS OF FINANCIAL ARRANGEMENTS CAN I MAKE IF I DECIDE TO PUT MY BABY UP FOR ADOPTION?

One thing you can't do is "sell" your baby; that is against the law. If someone offers to place your baby in a good home and provide quite a bit of money for you on the side, both of you will be breaking the law. By law, licensed agencies are allowed to charge a "reasonable" fee to cover the costs of their services. If one agency or individual has prices that are excessively high, beware. (This is good advice for adoptive parents, too.)

This does not mean that you have to bear the costs of having the baby alone. It is reasonable for the adoptive parents to provide for your pre- and post-natal care, hospitalization and doctor fees, medication charges, and other necessary expenses incurred as a result of the pregnancy. In some cases, this includes counseling, maternity clothes, and transportation to and from the doctor. It is *not* legal for them to pay you for having the baby. If you make an agreement to have the baby in exchange for receiving money, you should know that there is no way you can enforce that agreement.

The reason behind this law is that your consent to the adoption must be freely and voluntarily given before the court can enter the order of adoption. If you were to testify that you were desperate for money or were somehow bribed or coerced into agreeing to place the baby, the adoption could be declared invalid. The court would also declare the adoption invalid if you could show that you were unduly influenced or subjected to duress, fraud, or misrepresentation.

I HAD A BABY AND DECIDED TO KEEP IT, BUT IT'S JUST NOT WORKING OUT. CAN I PLACE A BABY WHO HAS ALREADY BEEN BORN UP FOR ADOPTION?

Yes, you can relinquish any child for adoption.[7] The law requires that the parent or parents show the judge that she or they fully and completely understand the significance of their relinquishment.

If you wanted to give up your child, you would file a petition of relinquishment in juvenile court, specifying that you believe it to be in the best interest of both yourself and the child. Relinquishment with respect to one parent does not affect the rights of the other parent. It would be advisable to seek advice from a lawyer or agency to file the proper documents. The judge may require you to do so or may appoint an attorney to assist you. The judge will ask you very specific questions to see if you understand what you're doing and why—chiefly, that in the eyes of the law, you will have no legal claim on or relationship with that child. If the judge is satisfied, he or she will enter an order terminating your rights as a parent. If you relinquish your child, the Department of Social Services or other agency will become the child's temporary guardian and custodian until, through its own agency, it places the child for adoption.

After the termination order is signed, your parental rights are permanently terminated. Unless you lodge an appeal within thirty days indicating that you had suffered undue influence, duress, fraud, or misrepresentation in agreeing to relinquish your child, the order will not be overturned and you will be forever deprived of your child. Even if you appeal, the higher court will only review the record of the proceedings to determine whether it shows that you knew and understood the significance of your action. It will not hear additional testimony.

You may also sign a written statement releasing your parental rights, duties, obligations, care, and control of your child to a licensed agency, thus surrendering the child for placement by that agency. The agency then becomes, in effect, the child's guardian until it is adopted.

WHAT ARE THE STEPS IN ADOPTION?

If you wish to adopt a child, you should start looking for a child by making contacts with various agencies or individuals who do adoptions. A good place to start is by contacting the Department of Social Services at 468-5400.

Initially, it must be determined that the child is legally free to be adopted, after which the child will be footprinted at the sheriff's office to conform to the Missing Children's Act. An attorney will then draw up the necessary legal documents.

Legally, adoption begins when a petition to adopt is filed in the juvenile court in the district in which the adoptive parents reside. If you are adopting the child, you must appear in court to establish the allegations in your petition. The child must also appear in court to consent to the adoption if he or she is over twelve in order to enable the judge to form an opinion about the child's best interests.

The judge does two things: he or she ascertains that the adoptive parents agree to treat the child as their own lawful child—to feed, clothe, educate, and support him or her and to perform all lawful duties toward him or her. The judge also ascertains that the biological parents freely give their consent for the adoption to take place. When the judge determines that the child's best interests are promoted by the adoption, he or she will issue an order approving the adoption. Once the order is issued, the adoptive child shall have all the rights of a natural child.

Usually the child's name is legally changed to that of the adoptive parents unless, in the case of an older child, he or she prefers his or her birth surname. In the case of an infant, a new birth certificate is issued which changes only the child's name and its parents' name. The child is given the same surname as its adoptive parents. No other information on the original birth certificate is modified.

Adoption-related matters can be handled in either juvenile court or the district court in which the adoptive parents reside. If a licensed agency has not also filed consent to the adoption, the court must—once a petition for adoption is filed—send a copy of the petition to the Division of Family Services within five days so that they can conduct their background investigation.[8]

The Division of Family Services then has sixty days to prepare its background report verifying the allegations of the petition and showing why the biological parents wish to be relieved of the care, support, and guardianship of the child; whether the biological parents have abandoned the child or are morally unfit to have its custody; whether the prospective parents are financially and morally fit to have the child; and any other circumstances which should be considered in the child's best interests.

If a licensed agency has been involved, the "agreement to release to the agency" and the agency's own investigative report are sufficient to enable the court to enter its order, since the agency acts as an arm of the state in conducting its investigation. No report is required from the Division of Family Services.

In the case of a non-agency adoption, the court may accept an affidavit of investigation from the adoptive parents' attorney or may waive investigation altogether.

An adoption petition cannot be granted (the step which makes it irrevocable) until the child has resided with the adoptive parents for a minimum of six months.

An agreement to adopt is legally enforceable if it is in writing, if the child's biological parents agree with the adoptive parents to relinquish their rights to the child in exchange for the adoptive parents' agreement to adopt, and if there is no intrinsic or extrinsic fraud, undue influence, or duress surrounding the consent to the adoption.

WHAT IF THE BIOLOGICAL PARENTS CHANGE THEIR MINDS?

While there is no law against a biological mother, for instance, changing her mind and revoking consent, the court will only look at the circumstances of the consent to see if it should be set aside. Since the original consent is given in court in the judge's presence or with persons licensed by the state as a child-placing agency, it is presumed to be valid and binding. The judge's finding of "knowing and voluntary consent" will not be overturned unless it appeared that the judge acted arbitrarily and capriciously in granting the adoption.

Grounds to revoke consent or to attack an adoption decree must be based on consent wrongfully obtained through fraud, misrepresentation, duress, or undue influence. Requiring that the biological mother or parents give consent is to protect their rights: they must be informed and fully understand the effect of giving consent for the adoption of their child.

CAN I GET COPIES OF THE ADOPTION PROCEEDINGS?

The petition, written investigative reports, and all other documents are sealed and cannot be inspected or copied without the express permission of the court for "good cause." Traditionally, "good cause" has been limited to mean the possibility of hereditary disease or some dire emergency. Curiosity is not sufficient. You must go back to court to get an order to unseal any adoption proceeding.

CHILD SUPPORT

WHAT IS CHILD SUPPORT?

Under the law, parents are responsible to support their children and provide for their care. If you have a child by a first marriage, your second husband is legally obligated to support that child as long as he is married to you. A stepparent shall support a stepchild to the same extent that a natural or adoptive parent is required to support a child.[9] However, the primary responsibility for child support rests with the biological parents (or with adoptive parents) and cannot be contracted away. Failing to support a child is a crime, punishable by jail and/or a fine. It can also be a civil offense, in case of divorce, since a court will have ordered support. Failure to pay can mean that you are in contempt of court and can be fined, jailed, or both.

If the parents are divorced, the court determines the amount of child support according to the child support guidelines[10] which came into effect July 1, 1989. These guidelines establish the amount of temporary or permanent child support that is to be contributed by both parents to the support of the child.

WHAT IF MY HUSBAND IS NOT PAYING CHILD SUPPORT?

If your husband has been ordered to pay support and does not do so, you can take him back to court, where he will be ordered to pay. If you cannot afford to hire a lawyer to help collect back child support, you can apply to the State Office of Recovery Services for help. This office has all the necessary forms and regulations you will need to proceed. Call 538-4400 in Salt Lake City to begin the process of opening a case.

Even if you are receiving some form of public assistance, the Office of Recovery Services will help you to collect your child support by getting court orders through the assistance of the county attorney's office for garnishment of wages or other orders which will require your husband to pay back child support. If your husband refuses or fails to pay the ordered support, he can be prosecuted and sentenced to jail.

In all divorces granted after November 1, 1990, child support obligations will be subject to automatic payroll withholding upon the request of one of the parties unless the divorce order contains a stipulation barring automatic withholding. In all cases, payroll withholding may be implemented if there is such justification for it as a pattern of irregular or short payments.

WHAT IF MY HUSBAND HAS LEFT THE STATE?

If you know where to locate him, you can still collect child support from your husband. URESA (the Uniform Reciprocal Enforcement of Support Act), passed in 1980, has eliminated conflicts between state laws and provides a means to enforce support obligations and collect judgments in other states.

Under URESA, unless you have a private attorney who will do it for you, the county attorney's office will forward the papers they give you to fill out to the appropriate state together with an affidavit stating the amount of child support owing, broken down month by month, and a certified copy of the divorce decree which shows the court-ordered amount. The law also empowers the Department of Social Services to garnishee wages and empowers the county attorney to divert tax returns for payment of support owing. Be aware that the process of filing on your husband and obtaining a judgment will probably take six months or more because of the backlog of cases.

WHAT IF I WANT TO CHANGE THE AMOUNT OF CHILD SUPPORT THAT MY HUSBAND IS PAYING?

The amount of child support may be modified if there is a material or substantial change in circumstances. The court will review the needs of the child and the parent's ability to pay. Affidavits substantiating the requested change, including both parents' income and expenses, must be submitted.

You begin the procedure by filing a motion for an order to show cause in district court. An order to show cause is served personally on your husband, specifying a date and time for a hearing. At the hearing, the judge will consider the request to modify the amount of child support in the original decree and the evidence supplied in your affidavits. The judge will adjust the amount if a material change in circumstances is shown.

If the original child support amount was set by another state, Utah will require that a petition for modification of the original divorce decree be filed. This will require that you obtain certified copies of your divorce papers from the state where you received your divorce.

WHEN DOES CHILD SUPPORT STOP?

Support stops when the child reaches the age of eighteen, unless both parties agree to extend support beyond that age for educational purposes or other reasons. You cannot agree to stop support before the age of eighteen.

CRIMES AGAINST CHILDREN

WHAT ARE CRIMES AGAINST CHILDREN?

As we have just mentioned, failing to support your children can be considered a crime. But what most often constitutes a crime against a child is abuse—physical, sexual, or emotional.

Crimes against children include encouraging, allowing, or compelling behavior that might contribute to a child's delinquency; willful abuse, neglect, or abandonment; kidnapping or enticing a child away from home or sheltering a runaway; or providing a child with alcohol or a controlled substance. The child need not be convicted of a delinquency before action can be taken against the adult in the case, and all of these actions can be prosecuted as crimes. The degree of crime and therefore the penalty will vary depending on the circumstances.[11]

To term these actions "crimes" means that they have a special legal status: the state has an interest in seeing that they do not occur and will act to protect the child. To remedy a *civil* offense, a "citizen" has to complain that his or her rights are being offended by the abuse. Since abuse can cause both emotional and physical injury, it is possible to sue the abuser for compensation, but this action must be taken by the person who was abused. In a *criminal* trial, the end result is to punish the offender and the state takes the initiative in prosecuting.

WHAT HAPPENS IF SOMEONE ABUSES A CHILD?

One of the sad things is that nearly always the abuse has to be so severe that someone notices it and reports it—a schoolteacher, a crossing guard, a neighbor who hears a child screaming and crying at night, or an emergency room attendant who becomes suspicious about certain types of injuries. Fortunately, in Utah it is a crime to know or suspect that a child is being abused or neglected and fail to report it to the police or to the Division of Family Services. The laws, in an effort to provide protection against abuse and neglect for children, specify molestation, incest, sexual exploitation, sexual abuse, physical abuse, and neglect.[12] Failure to report suspected abuse or neglect is a class B misdemeanor crime, which carries a sentence of up to six months in jail and/or a fine of $299.[13]

Generally speaking, neglect means that a child is not receiving "proper parental care" because the parent is not able to provide the child with the basic necessities of life such as necessary food, clothing, education, or medical care (including surgery or psychiatric service), and the care necessary for his or her emotional and moral well-being. Abuse means inflicting physical harm or injury on the child. 4

If you know or suspect abuse or neglect, you are required by law to notify the nearest policeman or law enforcement agency or the Department of Social Services. Any of them will investigate promptly (Social Services is required to investigate within seventy-two hours, for instance) and to keep your involvement confidential if you wish. If you notify Social Services and if it finds abuse, it is required to notify the police.[14]

If Social Services finds evidence of abuse or neglect, it will have the county attorney's office file a petition alleging abuse or neglect and asking the juvenile court to issue appropriate orders to correct the situation—for the parents to receive treatment, take parenting classes, receive therapy, etc. If the child is actually in danger, Social Services has legal authority to remove the child from the abusive or neglectful environment until the circumstances are corrected[15] and will ask the court to appoint a guardian for the child.

The parents receive a notice that the petition has been filed, complete with a hearing date. They are entitled to be represented by an attorney, court-appointed, if necessary, in these proceedings. They are also entitled to request a trial; the state is required to prove its allegations that abuse or neglect has occurred.[16]

If the parents admit their abuse or neglect or if the court finds sufficient evidence for abuse or neglect, it will enter its order requiring the parents to take treatment and to be accountable to the court, through Social Services, for improving the conditions of the child's environment.

This particular type of proceeding is not considered criminal, and the juvenile court judge does not have authority to jail or fine anyone. However, if the child or children have been removed from the home or if the court orders that they continue to stay in foster care while the parents receive treatment, the parents can be ordered to pay some or all of the costs of the care for the child outside the home.

In other cases, if a parent or other person brings an injured child to a doctor or hospital, the doctor or hospital may, by law, keep the child for up to seventy-two hours in protective custody if there is reason to suspect abuse or neglect and if, as well, there is reason to believe that the child's safety will be in danger without protective custody. Again, if a child is retained in protective custody, Social Services is immediately notified and a court order of temporary custody or protective supervision must be obtained to retain the child longer than seventy-two hours.

Even if the doctor or hospital does not exercise protective custody, Social Services must be notified of suspected abuse or neglect and can request follow-up written reports within forty-eight hours of the oral report.

Cases involving children can frequently involve two courts: the juvenile court, which has jurisdiction over actions involving abuse or neglect of children, and the criminal courts, which prosecute the offender.

All reports of suspected abuse or neglect are confidential and anyone who releases data or information obtained in the investigation can be charged with a class C criminal misdemeanor, which carries the penalty of ninety days in jail or a $299 fine or both.[17]

WHAT CRIMINAL PROCEDURES TAKE PLACE?

Many of the sexual crimes against children carry mandatory prison sentences. In these provisions, Utah law is similar to that of most states in the Union.

If a person has been charged with a felony involving a child sexually (for example, unlawful sexual intercourse, rape, object rape, sodomy, or sexual abuse), the penalties may include a minimum mandatory term of three, six, or nine years, or life imprisonment, if the crime was aggravated.[18]

However, Utah law is unique in that if certain conditions exist and the sexual offense involving the child is not considered legally to be ''aggravated,'' the court may suspend the prison sentence and impose probation and treatment instead.

These conditions are as follows:[19]

The defendant must be in a ''position of trust'' with the child, that is, a parent, stepparent, or legal guardian.

In the offense, the defendant acted alone, did not use weapons or force, and did not injure the child.

The defendant had no prior offenses involving sexual misconduct.

The offense did not involve pornography, prostitution, or sex with anyone else.

It is in the victim's best interests that the defendant not be imprisoned.

The defendant has been accepted for mental health treatment at a sexual abuse clinic and rehabilitation through treatment is probable.

The defendant will not live at home for one year.

The defendant will spend at least thirty days in jail and is on probation for a maximum of ten years.

I WAS SEXUALLY ABUSED BY MY STEPFATHER AS A CHILD BUT NO ONE EVER KNEW. AS AN ADULT, DO I HAVE ANY LEGAL RECOURSE OR RIGHT TO TREATMENT?

The law provides that you can file criminal charges only within one year of when you first learned about the abuse, not necessarily one year from the time it happened.

The cut-off point for filing a civil suit for emotional distress is two years from the time it occurred. Get advice from an attorney if you are unsure about your circumstances.

RIGHTS OF MINORS

HOW OLD DO I HAVE TO BE TO GET MARRIED?

In Utah, you have to be over eighteen or else have the permission of your parent or guardian to apply for a marriage license. (If you've been married before and are under eighteen, you are considered an adult in applying for a second marriage license.) If you are under sixteen and get married without parental consent, the marriage is not only illegal but is considered void from the beginning.

WHAT ABOUT GETTING AN ABORTION?

If you are under eighteen, you cannot receive contraceptive services or get an abortion from a publicly funded institution without the written consent of your parent or guardian unless you are married, a member of the armed forces, or otherwise emancipated. Emancipation means you have been declared independent either with or without the consent of parents or by the court.

For further discussion of these issues, see chapter 8, ''Physical and Mental Health.''

EDUCATION FOR HANDICAPPED

WHAT IS THE ''EDUCATION FOR ALL HANDICAPPED CHILDREN ACT''?

The Education for All Handicapped Children Act, commonly referred to as Public Law 94-142, guarantees every school-age handicapped child a free and ''appropriate'' public education.

Handicapped, according to the law, refers to the condition of a child who has a physical or mental disability that interferes with his or her ability to participate in or benefit from education programs. Examples include children who are hard of hearing or deaf, visually handicapped, mentally retarded, orthopedically impaired, learning disabled, speech impaired, autistic, or seriously emotionally disturbed.

Special education programs involve both specially designed instruction which will meet the unique educational needs of the child, and related services. These services include speech therapy, occupational therapy, counseling services, transportation, and any other support services needed to help the child participate in school.

Every school district must locate all handicapped children who live within the district, and every handicapped child must be given a complete evaluation to determine the extent of the child's handicap. Then, special education must be provided according to an individualized education plan (IEP). The IEP is the written plan that describes the child's educational program and is developed at a meeting among the parents, teacher, and an administrator from the child's school. Parents have an equal voice in developing their child's IEP.

If parents disagree with the school district's identification, evaluation, or placement of their child or if they believe that appropriate and necessary educational or related services are being denied, they may request a due-process hearing. An impartial hearing officer will be appointed to hear the evidence and determine if the child is receiving appropriate educational or related services.

If you have any questions concerning Public Law 94-142, you can call the Legal Center for People with Disabilities at 363-1347 or 1-800-662-9080.

5

HOUSING AND LANDLORD/TENANT RELATIONS

5

HOUSING OPTIONS AND ISSUES

INTRODUCTION

Options for housing are many and varied. They include owning a traditional home or condominium or paying rent for an apartment or home. Your choice of housing will depend upon your needs and financial resources. Each of these forms of housing has advantages and disadvantages, depending upon your circumstances and preferences. For example, if you own a traditional home you will be responsible for all maintenance and repairs, yard work, utility bills, taxes and insurance. By owning a condominium, you may retain a high degree of independence and privacy while avoiding the responsibilities of maintenance and yard work; however, you may also be liable for a periodic maintenance fee. By renting, you avoid responsibility for maintenance, mortgage payments, taxes, and insurance, but give up a degree of privacy and satisfaction of ownership. You should look for the form of housing that best meets your needs and resources.

INSURANCE

If you own a home, you should keep it adequately insured against loss by fire or other catastrophe. Insurance is generally required when there is a mortgage. For home insurance, you typically pay an annual premium that varies according to the amount of your deductible and the amount of your coverage. You may choose from standard insurance, which replaces your property up to a given value, or replacement insurance, which costs a little more but which guarantees replacement of your property regardless of the value.

PROPERTY TAX

Assessment and Payment

If you own real estate, taxes will be assessed on it that must be paid by November of each year. In the early summer, you will receive a valuation notice, telling you how much the county assessor has estimated your property to be worth. Your property taxes will then be calculated as a percentage of the estimated value of your property. Each autumn you will receive another notice to pay the tax. If you fail to pay it by November 30, your property will be sold by the county for the amount of the unpaid taxes plus penalties and interest. You may redeem your property from the tax sale by paying the amount due within five years. If you fail to do so, your property will be sold at an auction.

Reducing Property Taxes

There are some ways in which you can reduce your property taxes. One is to appeal the assessor's valuation of your property so that your taxes, which are a percentage of that value, will also be reduced. If you think your property is overvalued in the summer tax notice, you can contact your county commission's office and find out how to make an appeal. You will probably have to fill out forms and justify a reduction of the valuation of your property, which you can do by showing that comparable property recently sold for substantially less, or by having a private appraisal done showing a lower value.

You can also seek a reduction or deferral of your property taxes based on difficult financial circumstances, especially if you are over the age of sixty-five.

SELLING OR TRANSFERRING YOUR HOME

INTRODUCTION

Real estate is sold or transferred by means of a deed. Typically, a real estate agent or title company will assist you in selling your home and will take care of the necessary paperwork. If you sell your property to a new owner who becomes indebted to you for the purchase of your property, you should have the help of someone knowledgeable to protect your interest.

METHODS OF TRANSFERRING YOUR PROPERTY

The law provides a variety of ways in which you can transfer property while retaining partial control over it. For example, you can transfer your real estate but arrange for the transfer to take effect only at your death. It is also possible to arrange for a responsible person to take care of your property for you should you require it. In setting up arrangements like these, you should consult a lawyer. Although these arrangements are not overly complex, they need to be tailored to fit your specific situation.

AFFIDAVIT OF SURVIVORSHIP

Of course, you can transfer an interest only in property you actually own. Often married people own property jointly, with the survivor receiving full title to the property after the death of the spouse. This ownership arrangement is referred to as a ''joint tenancy.'' To find out whether you own your property in joint tenancy, look on the deed by which you received the property. If the deed reads, ''as joint tenants with right of survivorship'' or some close variant of that, then both of you own the property, with the survivor to retain full ownership when one of you dies.

If your spouse has died, then you, as the surviving joint owner of the property, need to show the death of your deceased spouse on the county records before you can transfer ownership of the house. You should contact your county recorder to obtain and file the proper form. The county recorder typically charges a filing fee.

If you need assistance with the transfer of your home, you should contact a lawyer.

AVOIDANCE OF TAX ON SALE OF HOME

If you have owned your home for many years, it is likely that the value of the home is substantially greater than when you purchased it. To relieve senior citizens of income tax liability for that increased value upon resale of their home, the tax laws allow a one-time exclusion of gain in the amount of $125,000. To qualify for the exclusion, the seller must be age fifty-five or older and must have owned and used the home as his or her principal residence for at least three of the previous five years. If the home is owned in joint tenancy by you and your spouse, at least one of you must satisfy the age and use requirements.

LANDLORD/TENANT RELATIONS

INTRODUCTION

If you live in a rented residence, you have rights that are specified either in a written "lease" or in an unwritten understanding between your landlord (the owner of the property) and you, the renter (or tenant). It is best to have a written lease so that you can refer back to it if a dispute should arise.

LEASE PROVISIONS

The central purpose of your lease is to allow you to occupy the leased property in return for paying rent to your landlord. The lease usually covers other aspects of your relationship with your landlord, including a provision describing when and how the lease will end. Here is a checklist of things to look for in a lease:

Rent

The lease should clearly set forth how much rent you must pay, along with when, how, where, and to whom it is to be paid. It should also state whether your landlord will charge you a late fee if your rent is not paid on time.

Term

Your lease should expressly state its term, or how long it is to run. Also, your lease should state whether and under what conditions it can be renewed. Further, your lease should contain a provision about whether either you or your landlord may cancel or modify it prior to its expiration. It should explain any procedures that must be followed in the event of cancellation or modification.

Deposits

When entering into a lease you may be required to make a deposit. If your landlord requires a deposit, your lease should include all pertinent information about this deposit, including its amount, its purpose, and the time and conditions of a refund. If the deposit is designed to protect the landlord against damage you may cause to the property, you should make a list of all existing damage before moving in and have the landlord sign and date the list.

Utilities

The lease should state which utilities your landlord will pay and which you must pay. If the rented property is located in a water or sewer district, it is advisable that the landlord pay those utilities because nonpayment may result in a tax sale of the property.

Landlord's Right to Enter Premises

The lease should state whether the landlord has the right to enter your rented premises during the period of your lease and what control he can exercise over the property.

Tenant's Right to Use Rented Premises

The lease should also describe what rights you have to the use of the premises. It should say whether you may keep pets, have other persons live with you, or sublease the apartment to another person during the term of your original lease.

Repairs

Under current Utah law, landlords are responsible for maintaining a residential rental unit in a condition fit for human habitation. Landlords are prohibited from renting a residential unit that is not "safe, sanitary and fit for human occupancy."[1] Each residential unit is required to have an electrical system, heating, plumbing, and hot and cold water.

Your landlord also has a duty[2] to: (1) maintain the common areas of your rental unit in a safe and sanitary condition; (2) maintain plumbing, electrical systems, heating, and hot and cold water; (3) maintain other appliances and facilities as specifically provided in your lease agreement; and (4) if your rental unit is in a building containing at least one or more other rental units, your landlord must provide and maintain appropriate garbage receptacles and arrange for garbage removal.

If you believe that your health or safety is affected by the condition of your rental unit, you are required to give written notice to your landlord. Within a reasonable time after having reviewed the notice, your landlord should begin action to correct the conditions about which you have complained. However, your landlord is under no obligation to remedy conditions caused by you, your family, or your guests.

The landlord may refuse to correct the condition and may terminate your lease if your unit is unfit for occupancy. If your landlord terminates your lease, he or she must notify you in writing. If your lease agreement is terminated, the rent you have already paid shall be refunded for the days you paid for that extend beyond the termination date. However, you may not be required to leave your residence sooner than ten days after your landlord gives you notice.

As a renter, you also have specific duties with regard to your rental property.[3] You are required to (1) comply with the rules of your local board of health that materially affect your physical health and safety and that of others sharing common areas; (2) maintain your rental unit in a clean and safe condition; (3) refrain from unreasonably obstructing common areas; (4) dispose of all garbage and waste in a clean and safe manner; (5) maintain plumbing fixtures in as sanitary a condition as possible; (6) refrain from increasing the number of permanent occupants of your rental unit without the landlord's permission; (7) pay your rent when it is due; and (8) comply with your lease agreement. You may not damage or remove any part of your rental unit or allow others to do so, or unreasonably deny consent to your landlord to enter your rental unit for the purpose of making repairs. You must also respect the peaceful enjoyment of neighboring tenants.

You should also be aware that any of the duties outlined above may be allocated to a different party by a written agreement signed by the landlord and renter.

If a reasonable time elapses after you serve the written notice on your landlord and the condition or problem has still not been corrected, you may serve a "Notice to Repair or Correct Condition" on your landlord. This notice must (1) mention the first notice sent; (2) state the number of days that have gone by with no action by your landlord; (3) state the conditions that have not been corrected; (4) demand that these conditions be corrected; and (5) state that if corrective action is not begun within three days, you will take the landlord to court.

You may be entitled to damages and injunctive relief if you can
5 show that your landlord failed to use due diligence to correct the condition or problem.[4]

WHAT TO WATCH OUT FOR

You should try to avoid signing a lease form provided by a landlord that contains a provision that (1) relieves the landlord of responsibility for repairs; (2) makes the tenant responsible for repairs, even if the tenant is not at fault; (3) gives the landlord the right to enter rented premises at unreasonable times; (4) makes future rent payments due immediately in the event of the tenant's breach of the lease; (5) relieves the landlord of liability to the tenant for personal injury or property damage caused by the landlord's negligence or by any other cause related to the security or condition of the property; or (6) requires the tenant to accept the premises "as is," particularly when there is not opportunity to inspect the premises.

In case of a service dispute, you should see an attorney. Self-help measures may create more trouble. Your landlord cannot legally change the locks and refuse to give you a key, move or take possession of your property, break into the rented property, or attempt to use force of any kind.

EVICTION

To evict you, your landlord must give you a "Notice to Quit." If you receive a "Notice to Quit" after having broken the requirements of your lease, for example by not paying rent, you will generally be required to leave unless you correct the problem. The landlord cannot remove you from the rental property without filing a summons and complaint and obtaining a court order for eviction. However, if you are in violation of the lease, you may be required to pay triple rent beginning three days after you receive the notice to quit. If you are renting on a month-to-month basis, the landlord may evict you for no cause by giving fifteen days' notice. (This does not apply to government-subsidized housing.)

REFUND OF DEPOSIT

Any refundable deposit must be returned to the tenant within thirty days from the end of the lease term, or else the tenant must be given a written itemization of how the deposit was spent to cover authorized expenses. If the deposit is not refunded or the tenant disagrees with how the deposit was spent by the landlord, the tenant may bring an action in small claims court to recover the deposit. If you feel you are being treated unfairly or are the victim of an illegal action, you should consult a lawyer.

6

PROPERTY RIGHTS AND THE MAKING OF A WILL

IF I AM MARRIED, CAN I MAKE DECISIONS ABOUT MY PROPERTY AS I PLEASE?

The law generally has two categories of property. ''Real'' property, roughly, is ''unmovable'' property such as land and buildings (hence the term ''real estate''), while personal property is ''movable'' and includes clothing, jewelry, money, stocks and bonds, etc. If you own property, you have certain legal rights and obligations. If you wish, you may sell, give, or will your property to someone else.

Historically, women have been given fewer property rights than men; however, Utah law has never recognized the ''common law'' idea that married women are incapable of owning their own property.[1] Laws passed in Utah, before it became a state in 1896, denied the traditional ''incapacity'' of married women to hold property.[2] Utah's constitution provides that any property a woman acquires before or during marriage is part of her own estate and cannot be used without her permission by anyone, even to pay her husband's debts;[3] she can make decisions about what happens to her property ''as if she were unmarried.''[4] Utah law also gives married women the right to hold separate real and personal property.[5] Further, if a husband acquires possession or control of his wife's property, she has the right to sue him as if they were not married.[6] A spouse, however, can give to or get from the other spouse a written power of attorney that allows her or him to dispose of his or her property.[7]

WHAT ARE THE LIMITATIONS ON A MARRIED WOMAN'S RIGHTS TO PROPERTY SEPARATE FROM HER HUSBAND'S?

Utah law allows any debts that come from "expenses of the family and the education of the children" to be charged against (or paid by) the property of a husband and/or wife.[8]

The rights given to women also are given to men, which means that if a husband acquires property with his own money and keeps title to that property in his name, Utah law gives him all rights of ownership to that property, including the rights to sell, bequeath in a will, and to use the value of that property to pay his debts.

WHAT PROPERTY RIGHTS DO I HAVE IF MY HUSBAND DIES?

The nature and amount of an interest you can claim in the property of your spouse depends upon when he died and whether he considered Utah his home at the time of his death.

In 1975, the Utah legislature changed former laws dealing with succession (who receives what on death) and gave a widow or widower the right to choose an "elective share" of a spouse's estate.[9] To be eligible for such a share you must have been married to someone who considered Utah his home.[10] If he did, you can claim the elective share *instead* of what was actually designated in your spouse's will.[11]

The elective share statute provides a complicated formula for determining the actual share of the estate to which you are entitled. Basically, it gives you one-third of the estate after funeral expenses and outstanding bills are paid, multiplied by a fraction based on the relationship of the marital property to the estate after bills have been paid. An attorney can help you identify the legal value of the property you shared with your husband and what your legal share is after his death. The details regarding what property can actually be included in your spouse's estate are very complex. A lawyer can help clarify them.

If, after your spouse's death, you think you might want to choose an elective share rather than the property identified in your husband's will, you must obtain legal advice.

WHAT IS A WILL?

A will is a written document in which you declare your wishes for the disposal of your property, both real and personal, upon your death. A will does not become effective until you die. All property in which you have an interest at your death becomes your "estate." You should prepare a will regardless of how much or how little property or money you have. Otherwise, property that is not automatically disposed of by a contract, such as life insurance, passes to your survivors by an inflexible formula fixed by law. (This process is described below in the section on dying intestate.) Those who are named in a will to receive an inheritance are called heirs.

It is generally recommended that you have an attorney prepare your will, because there are certain legal formalities that must be observed for the will to be "probated" after your death. "Probate" is the process by which a will is accepted by a court as the last legal statement of the deceased's intentions for distribution of the estate.

HOW DO I KNOW IF MY WILL IS VALID?

To create a valid will, you must be mentally competent, at least eighteen years old, intend the will to distribute your property at the time of your death, and not be unduly influenced or defrauded by others.

In addition, a formal will must be in writing, signed by you (the "testator"), and signed by at least two "disinterested" witnesses who are at least eighteen years of age.[12] The "witnesses" must watch you sign the will and must sign in each other's presence. A witness can receive property under the terms of the will and still be disinterested if he or she receives less than he or she would if you died without making a will. Generally, it is better to get witnesses who do not receive property under the will. If you are unable to sign your will, someone else may sign for you, but only at your request and direction.[13] It is best to sign at the end of the will so that nothing can be added by another person. In some states three witnesses are required, so you may want to avoid difficulties that could arise if you move out of state by obtaining the signatures of three witnesses.

The final form a valid will may take in Utah is one written by the person making the will. This type of will is called a "holographic" (handwritten) will. To be valid, a holographic will must have the parts of the will that give property to people written in the will-maker's own handwriting. It does not need to be witnessed by anyone else,[14] and it should be clearly signed and dated.

Oral wills, even those made at death, are not recognized in Utah. It is very important that you protect your right to distribute your property by consulting an attorney and creating a will.

WHAT DOES A WILL DO?

Your intentions for the disposition of your property, as expressed in your will, will be followed as closely as possible. With few limitations, you may leave your property in any manner and to anyone you choose. The major exception to this rule is designed to help the surviving spouse. He or she has the option of accepting the share of the estate left by the will or of renouncing the will and choosing to take the elective share described earlier.

CAN PROPERTY BE TRANSFERRED AT DEATH BY MEANS OTHER THAN A WILL?

Most contracts which are intended to pass property upon the death of one of the persons involved cannot be legally enforced. Notable exceptions are life insurance policies and pension funds.

A joint account in your name and the name of another person, including your spouse, which is payable to either person or to the survivor if one dies, will permit the surviving person to keep the money in the account.[15] Accounts can also be designated POD (pay on death).

You can create an account in your name "in trust" for another person who is known as a beneficiary.[16] "In trust" simply means that you are giving the money to the beneficiary but are retaining control over the administration of the funds. After your death, that person may withdraw the money.[17]

Finally, real property (basically land and buildings) can be owned by two people in what is called joint tenancy. Joint tenancy means that if one person dies, the surviving owner owns the entire property. Joint tenants need not be married.

WHAT DOES "INTESTATE" MEAN?

When you die without leaving a will, you die "intestate," literally, without a legal will or testament. The intestate estate is the total property of the person who died without a will, except property that is transferred by insurance contract, joint account, trust, or joint tenancy.

Utah law specifically describes which relatives will inherit what property if someone dies without a legal will.

IF MY HUSBAND DIES INTESTATE, WHAT DO I INHERIT?

Your inheritance depends on the circumstances. If there are no surviving children or parents of your dead spouse, the entire intestate estate is yours. If there are no surviving children of your spouse but his parents are still alive, the first $100,000, plus one-half of the balance of the intestate estate, belongs to you. If there are surviving children who are also your children, the first $50,000, plus one-half of the balance of the intestate estate, is yours. If there are surviving children but one or more of them are not your children, you inherit one-half of the intestate estate.[18]

ARE THERE OTHER QUALIFICATIONS TO INHERIT PART OF THE INTESTATE ESTATE?

Utah law says that any heir receiving property through intestacy—that is, without a legal will—must survive the decedent by 120 hours.[19] Also, the decedent's relatives of half blood inherit as if they were of whole blood.[20] A "half blood" relative is related to the deceased by only one common ancestor, rather than two; for example, you are a child of the deceased's mother but not of the deceased's father. In addition, relatives of the decedent who were conceived before, but born after, death, inherit as if they had been born at the time the decedent died.[21] It does not matter if the heir, or the person through whom the heir inherits, is a citizen of the United States.[22]

For purposes of intestate succession, an adopted person is considered to be the biological child of the adopting parents.[23] An illegitimate child is considered a child of the mother only, unless the parents were married at the time of birth but the marriage was later declared void, or paternity (fatherhood) is established by a court.[24] Generally, fatherhood must be legally established before death. The requirements to obtain a declaration of paternity after death are much more strict. Accordingly, steps should be taken before death to have a court issue a declaration of paternity.

BEFORE I MARRY, CAN I ENTER INTO AN AGREEMENT WITH MY FUTURE HUSBAND ABOUT OWNERSHIP OF PROPERTY?

Yes. An agreement that you make with your prospective spouse is called a prenuptial or antenuptial agreement. There are many reasons for making such an agreement. First, it requires that you discuss each person's assets and liabilities. In fact, it is essential that both of you know and understand the extent of property, debts, and income of the other to obtain a valid prenuptial agreement. Second, you may wish to retain separate property after the marriage and later decide to give that property to someone other than your spouse. In an antenuptial agreement, your future husband can renounce or deny any claim to that property. Third, you could obtain a position where you earn more money than your husband. If this happens and you later divorce, the law may require you to pay alimony to your husband. Either a husband or wife can waive any claim to alimony in a prenuptial agreement.

A valid prenuptial agreement must meet certain requirements. Both people must completely disclose their assets and liabilities. The agreement must be in writing, signed by each person, and the signatures notarized. Neither person can be subjected to undue influence—that is, neither can be forced, threatened, or bribed to sign the document. If the value, extent, or ownership of property has been misrepresented, the agreement could be rendered void.[25]

When you think about preparing a prenuptial agreement, you should be absolutely certain that your intended husband is being completely honest in his disclosures. You should not sign the agreement until you understand all of its terms and conditions. A prenuptial or antenuptial agreement is a very important document. If you have any questions, do not hesitate to seek advice from a third party, preferably an attorney.

7

UTAH MARRIAGE AND DIVORCE LAW

WHAT IS THE LEGAL AGE FOR MARRIAGE IN UTAH?

In Utah, a man or woman under the age of fourteen cannot legally marry. If either a man or woman is under the age of sixteen, a marriage between them is void and considered of no force unless the person under sixteen received parental permission.[1] When a marriage license is issued, the parties are required to present proof of their age. If either party is under eighteen, he or she must present a special permission form bearing the notarized signature of a parent or guardian; failure to obtain permission is grounds for annulment.

In Utah, men or women of the age of eighteen or over may marry without parental permission.[2]

WHAT IF I AM ABUSED BY MY SPOUSE?

You and your spouse can be helped. The 1990 Utah Legislature adopted tough laws addressing the problem of domestic violence. Police officers are required to arrest or cite individuals for certain acts of domestic violence. The law provides for treatment programs and services related to such abuse, and there is a mandatory twenty-four-hour "no contact" period after an incident of domestic violence. Trial programs using this approach have shown that, through proper treatment, abusive behavior can be changed. (As this handbook went to press, the new laws were being challenged as unconstitutional. Call the police department or an attorney if you are being abused and want to know how the law can help you.)

HOW DO I START DIVORCE PROCEEDINGS?

Since marriage is a legal contract, sanctioned by the state, its dissolution is also a legal matter. When either wife or husband feels that the terms of the marriage contract have been broken, either one can file for divorce in the state district court of the county in which either has resided for the last three months.[3] (Every state has a residency requirement. Utah's is in the middle, between Nevada's six weeks and California's six months.)

Utah law allows divorce for irreconcilable differences. "Irreconcilable differences" means that, for one reason or another, you believe your marriage cannot continue. You do not have to allege that your spouse is at fault. This is a form of no-fault divorce.

WHAT HAPPENS IN DIVORCE PROCEEDINGS?

We will describe the procedure as if you were filing for a divorce, making you the plaintiff and your husband the defendant. (If your husband were to file, you would be the defendant and he would be the plaintiff.) For the legal divorce process to begin, you must file a complaint with the clerk of the court.

The terms of the complaint are drafted by your attorney based on your answers to questions such as these: How much support do you need? What share of the property do you want or do you think would be fair? What is your husband's income? Is alimony appropriate?

The current filing fee is $77. If you believe you cannot afford to pay $77, you can ask your attorney (or the clerk of the court, if you are representing yourself) for an "Affidavit of Impecuniosity." This affidavit simply states that you believe you cannot afford to pay the filing fee. You can also include a request in your complaint for the court to order your husband to reimburse you for the $77. The complaint sets forth the factual situation and the reasons for the divorce, the agreements you and your husband have already made, if any (about custody and property, for instance), and the other items that must be resolved between the parties.

Next, your husband must be given "notice" (a summons) of the divorce action. In the case of formal notice, the sheriff or constable may serve (personally hand-deliver) the notice to your husband. In informal service, your lawyer may mail a copy to your husband, informing him of the action and enclosing a copy of the complaint. In formal service, your husband has twenty days to file an "answer" or propose a compromise or modification. With informal service, he must respond within a reasonable time or be formally served. The answer sets out what the defendant agrees and disagrees with. Often an answer and counterclaim are filed simultaneously. A counterclaim is a counter-suit. In it your husband says, "Wait. I deserve a divorce from *you*." In the answer and/or counterclaim, he sets forth the manner in which *he*
7 thinks the issues should be resolved about custody of children, support, property division, etc.

In response to a counterclaim, your attorney will file a reply, which is the equivalent of your husband's answer: you agree with certain statements in his counterclaim and disagree with others.

Under no circumstances should you attempt to deal with a divorce without at least consulting a lawyer. Even if you think you agree to all of the terms in the complaint, you can benefit from the experience of someone who knows the process. If your husband has had his complaint served formally, it is essential that you have an attorney. Formal service almost always means that your husband is planning to be aggressive and uncooperative.

If your husband wants to contest (disagree with) the terms of the divorce and files an answer which you believe is unreasonable or unfair and to which you cannot agree, the matter goes to trial. At a trial, all of the facts are presented to the judge, who makes the final decision as to whether a divorce should be granted, who should get custody, whether alimony should be awarded and, if so, what amount, what amount of child support should be ordered, who gets what property, etc.

Before a contested divorce goes to trial, both lawyers will engage in "discovery." Discovery is a method of "discovering" facts and information about the litigation and the other side's position. For instance, your husband might want to find out about your retirement plan and how much it is worth, in which case he would subpoena the retirement records from your employer. You might want to find out more about the partnership your husband is involved in; you would subpoena the records from that business for your attorney to review. If there is a fight over custody, discovery usually involves a "custody evaluation"—a home study and review by a social worker, psychologist, or other professional, who makes an expert recommendation to the court concerning who can best care for the children.

Once both parties have had a chance to do "discovery," a process that usually takes several months, the matter is presented to the judge at a trial. After hearing all of the facts, the judge then makes a decision about every item in dispute. That final decision is embodied in a written legal document known as the decree. The decree is the final order that legally terminates the marriage and resolves the various disputes.

Many times the parties can agree on and resolve certain disputes before the trial—for example, that Janet will have custody of the five children—but cannot agree on related issues. How much child support should Jay pay? Should Janet have possession of the house until the youngest child reaches the age of eighteen? Each person tells the judge at the beginning of the trial exactly what is in dispute and the court directs its attention only to those items.

Over 95 percent of the divorces in Utah do *not* go to trial. Most divorces are either uncontested or negotiated and settled before trial, but you *will* need a lawyer. Although both of you may want a divorce, it is still a legal matter.

In a simple, uncontested divorce, you (if you are the plaintiff) file the divorce action and deliver a copy of the complaint to your husband. He reviews the complaint and finds that he can agree to all of the terms. He then signs a short legal document variously called an acceptance, waiver, or consent before a notary public. The acceptance declares that the defendant accepts and agrees to the terms as set forth in the complaint. The signed and notarized acceptance is filed with the court. The court then allows you to present grounds, etc., and to be granted the divorce.

In a more complicated no-trial divorce, your husband may not agree to all of the terms in the complaint. Negotiations begin, with or without filing an answer. Negotiations would be along the lines of "If you get the car, then I want a greater portion of the equity on the house," or "If you get the rental property, then I want the difference made up in my alimony payments."

These negotiations may go on for months and may result in the parties being able to reach a written agreement or "settlement stipulation" resolving all the disputed items. If that is the case, the plaintiff will go to court, present the settlement along with grounds, etc., and the court will grant the divorce in the same manner as an uncontested divorce.

This negotiation process may also result in the resolution of many issues before trial, but leave a few issues you cannot agree on for the judge to consider. Sometimes these negotiations result in a settlement right at the courthouse door, just before trial.

Most divorce attorneys will work hard to negotiate and settle a case before trial. The judge's decision is usually "fair" (a forced compromise) from the view of a disinterested third party, but a negotiated settlement is usually better because it means that you can be involved in developing your own compromise.

After a divorce action (the complaint) has been filed, it is considered pending until there can be a hearing. Since you must usually wait three months (a period set by law) before even a "default" hearing (appearing before the judge to present grounds orally), it is often necessary to seek a temporary order regarding custody, child support, etc.

WHAT ARE THE GROUNDS FOR DIVORCE IN UTAH?

Utah law allows divorce for "irreconcilable difference." This means you do not have to assign blame and can simply tell the court that the marriage is no longer working. Thus "irreconcilable differences" means whatever the parties want it to mean.

One advantage to "irreconcilable differences" as grounds is that you don't have to reveal to a judge or to the court why you want your marriage dissolved; those reasons are really no one else's business.

The state didn't ask you why you wanted to get married. The state should not ask you why you want to terminate your marriage.

Other grounds for divorce in Utah include the following:

Impotency at the time of marriage.

Adultery committed after the marriage.

Desertion of the spouse for more than one year.

Failure to provide the "common necessities of life." This means, basically, refusal to support you. This ground is established if your husband moves out and you have to seek public assistance. Because of the fault concept used in Utah, this ground would probably require that your husband have the ability to support you but fail to do so. If he were physically disabled, for instance, and could not support the family, this ground would probably not apply.

Habitual drunkenness. This conduct also overlaps with the category of "mental cruelty"; thus, there is no need to be specific. If you can say, "My husband has used alcohol to excess" or "My husband's consumption of alcohol creates problems between us," that constitutes mental cruelty.

Conviction or being found guilty of a felony, a serious crime for which a person can be sentenced to prison for more than one year. Examples are murder, rape, burglary, robbery, possession or sale of large quantities of illicit drugs, etc.

Mental or physical cruelty, that is, cruel treatment that causes bodily injury or great mental distress.

Legal separation by a court decree for three consecutive years. A legal separation or separate maintenance decree is described later.

Permanent and incurable insanity, which must be established by actual court-ordered commitment to a hospital or by competent medical testimony.

WHAT IS THE DIFFERENCE BETWEEN A LEGAL SEPARATION AND A DIVORCE IN UTAH?

Parties are "legally separated" only when a court has entered a decree of separate maintenance, a court order which divides property, provides support, etc. Based upon a determination by the parties that they cannot live together, the court enters an order to resolve questions of property, support, etc., without terminating the marriage. The order requires that the parties live separately, specifies who gets what property, who pays what support, which party is responsible for which bills, which children will live with which parent, etc.[4]

To obtain a decree of separate maintenance in Utah, a couple must go through a proceeding very much like a divorce. A decree of separate maintenance divides property, awards custody of children, and provides for child support and alimony—but only for a temporary period of time. A decree of separate maintenance may stay in effect until the death of either party or until one or the other seeks a divorce. There is no limit to its duration.

A decree of separate maintenance does not legally end a marriage. Alimony is more common under a decree of separate maintenance than under a divorce decree because the parties are still legally married, and the law requires that a husband support his wife.

The paper work, attorney's fees, and court costs for a legal separation are about the same as for a divorce. If, after a legal separation is decreed, a couple decides they want a divorce, additional attorney's fees and court fees must be paid for the divorce. However, living under a decree of separate maintenance for three years is grounds for divorce.

Some women prefer a legal separation to a divorce because a legal separation may enable them to stay on their husbands' health insurance policies and may enable them to retain their inheritance rights. It is best to check with a lawyer and with your insurance company if these are the reasons you want a legal separation instead of a divorce.

HOW DO I GET A LEGAL SEPARATION IN UTAH?

You hire an attorney to file a complaint for a legal separation, just as you would for a divorce. In Utah, the statutory grounds for separate maintenance are the same for both men and women and include the following:

A spouse has deserted you without good and sufficient cause, or

He could support you but either neglected or refused to ''properly provide for and suitably maintain'' you, or

He lives away from you through no fault of yours, or

He is sentenced to the state prison for a year or more.

There is no three-month residency requirement to seek a decree of separate maintenance in Utah, but you must be a resident of the state (of no specific duration).[5]

WHAT ARE THE LEGAL REASONS FOR AN ANNULMENT IN UTAH?

An annulment is a court decision that a marriage was not valid at the time it took place. It means the marriage never existed legally, unlike a divorce which dissolves a previously legal and valid marriage.[6]

The two most common grounds for annulment are ''lack of capacity'' and fraud. ''Lack of capacity'' means that for some reason a person was legally incapable of marrying—he or she was under legal age, or still married to another person, mentally defective, or so drunk that he or she didn't know what he or she was doing.

To prove that one of these conditions existed, a court will sometimes accept your husband's admission. For instance, if he is served with the complaint for an annulment and he does not respond or deny the grounds, his lack of action constitutes agreement to the annulment. Proof that a previous divorce was not final could be given by showing the court a copy of the decree. Proof that he was under age and did not have parental permission could be shown by a copy of a birth certificate and a copy of the marriage license without a parent's signature.

Proof that a person was incapacitated and not acting in awareness could come from her own testimony; for instance, ''We had been drinking for three days and taking pills. I remember going to Elko but can't remember anything after that. When we got back to Salt Lake and

I sobered up, Lawrence told me we were married and showed me a marriage license.''

Fraud as grounds for annulment must be a ''substantial and material untruth'' which actually affects someone's decision to marry. If a person conceals the fact of several previous marriages or if a woman tells her prospective husband she is pregnant with his child when she is not, fraud is involved.

Another reason for annulment is kinship. If parties are cousins or ''closer,'' the marriage is incestuous and void. Uncle and niece are ''closer,'' and so are ''blood''-related brothers and sisters, and half-brothers and half-sisters.[7]

Other grounds for annulment in Utah are that a spouse has a communicable venereal disease or AIDS or that the marriage ceremony was not performed by an authorized person.[8]

WHAT ARE THE RESIDENCE REQUIREMENTS FOR A DIVORCE IN UTAH?

A divorce action can be started in any Utah county in which either spouse has been a resident for *at least three months* immediately before the filing of the divorce action with the court.

By law, there can be no final court action on a divorce until at least ninety days have passed from the date of the filing of the action. The judge, however, does have the discretion to shorten the waiting period. If you make such a request, you will need to present the judge with proof (such as an affidavit from your psychologist) stating that you have had sufficient time to think about your decision to divorce and that shortening the time period would be in your best interest. Utah divorce law requires this ''cooling-off period'' in the hope that the couple may reconcile.

After the judge signs the decree and it is noted in court records, the divorce becomes final without any further action by the husband, the wife, or the court. There is no longer a waiting period between the time the divorce is granted and the date it becomes final.[9]

There are no durational residency requirements or waiting periods for annulments or legal separations, but the person who starts one of these legal actions must live in Utah, i.e., be a resident (have an intent to continue to live in Utah indefinitely) to apply for separate maintenance, or have a domicile (be living in Utah) to apply for an annulment.

There are no waiting periods for annulment or separate maintenance actions. If you moved to Utah today, filed an action for an annulment or legal separation tomorrow, and if you and your husband agreed on all terms, the action could be final within weeks.

HOW MUCH WILL A DIVORCE COST IN UTAH?

The average attorney's fee for a simple, uncontested divorce in Utah is between $125 and $400. In addition there are court costs, i.e., filing fees ($77), and sheriff's fees (usually between $25 and $35).

In an uncontested simple divorce, the only court cost is the filing fee. If it remains uncontested, the papers are simply mailed. Thus the only cost is the filing fee of $77. Even this fee can be waived if you file an "Affidavit of Impecuniosity" and if you can convince the judge that your income is low enough that you cannot afford to pay the filing fee. 7

If a spouse decides to fight or contest a divorce and goes through a full trial, the attorney's fees will increase and will probably be figured on an hourly basis. Hourly fees vary widely, but usually fall between $50 and $125 per hour. A young attorney will work for $50 to $60 an hour just to keep busy, while a seasoned veteran will charge $100-plus per hour. If a divorce is contested, both sides will have to pay similar attorney's fees.

Utah law stipulates that if either spouse cannot afford an attorney in a divorce action, he or she may ask the judge to order the other spouse to pay the attorney's fees and the court costs.

CAN MY HUSBAND STOP ME FROM GETTING A DIVORCE?

No, one spouse cannot prevent the other from getting a divorce. But your husband can slow the process down. When someone contests a divorce, the disagreement usually involves finances, support, custody of children, or property division. Usually both spouses agree that there should be a divorce but disagree on its terms. By contesting a divorce, the defendant does not prevent it but simply prolongs the process. In Utah, a contested divorce usually takes much longer than the usual three months for an uncontested divorce. It will require a minimum of three months, and could be more than a year, because of the need for "discovery" and the court's crowded calendar.

WHAT IF MY HUSBAND WON'T ACCEPT THE DIVORCE PAPERS?

Your husband does not have to sign and agree to the terms of the divorce complaint for the divorce to proceed. If he will not voluntarily receive a copy of the complaint and does not file an answer or other response with the court, he can be served formally by a sheriff or constable. Upon formal service, if the defendant does not respond within twenty days (by filing an answer or other legal written response with the clerk of the court), he loses and you are granted (or given) everything you asked for in the complaint. Thus, a divorce can proceed even if the defendant will not cooperate by responding to the papers after being informally served.

WHAT HAPPENS IF THE DEFENDANT DOES NOT RESPOND IN ANY WAY TO THE DIVORCE PAPERS?

If your husband receives the divorce complaint and summons through formal service but does not file any papers to answer or fight, the divorce will be granted exactly as you have asked. The judge will not usually question the reasonable division of property, custody, child support, or alimony in your divorce complaint unless there is a response of some sort from the defendant.

If a spouse feels that there are errors or unfair requests in the divorce complaint, he or she should answer or challenge those items.

After a divorce has been granted, it is difficult to change the terms. If you want to argue about any part of the divorce, it is best to do so while the divorce action is still in process. To change something later, the defending spouse must show a *substantial* change in circumstances.

Even though it may seem difficult to hire a lawyer, it is best to consult one to protect your interests while the divorce action is still in process, rather than after the divorce has been granted.

IF MY HUSBAND DOES NOT LIVE IN UTAH, CAN I GET A DIVORCE HERE?

The key to where a divorce can be granted is *jurisdiction*. Jurisdiction simply means that the court has power over the case. Utah law says that if there is a "substantial connection" between the parties, the marriage, and the State of Utah, and the other spouse has been informed in writing of the proceedings, a Utah court can grant a divorce.

A "substantial connection" means that the parties lived together in Utah during the marriage or that the acts constituting the grounds for divorce occurred in Utah (for example, if your husband beat and abandoned you while the two of you were passing through Utah). You should ask an attorney for an opinion regarding your individual case.

If you are a resident of Utah and your husband has never been in Utah, a Utah court can grant a divorce and award custody of children in Utah, but it *cannot* order him to pay child support, alimony, or attorney's fees, nor can it divide the property acquired during the marriage unless he agrees.

CAN I GET A DIVORCE EVEN IF I DON'T KNOW WHERE MY HUSBAND IS LIVING?

Yes, you can get a divorce even though your husband cannot be found. If, after you make a diligent search, you cannot find him so that he can be personally served with divorce papers, the court will proceed with the divorce action by giving permission to publish notice of the divorce action in a newspaper and/or to mail notice to the spouse's last known address or to the address of relatives. A divorce granted in this way is restricted to terminating the marriage, granting custody of the children who are in Utah, and dividing property in Utah. The court cannot make any decision about property outside of Utah, child support, attorney's fees, or alimony in a divorce where notice is given by publication or by mail.

DO I HAVE TO ATTEND COUNSELING BEFORE I FILE FOR A DIVORCE?

Technically, under Utah law, the court *may* require some marriage counseling before a divorce is granted. The purpose of the counseling is twofold: to ascertain whether the marriage can be held together and, if not, to help prepare the wife and husband for their new roles as unmarrieds. Salt Lake County no longer requires counseling.

Getting a divorce is an emotionally taxing experience for most people, especially when children are involved. An attorney can provide only legal advice, and a court can resolve only legal matters. Although it is not a legal requirement, you may wish to seek counseling to help you cope with the emotional and psychological aspects of divorce.

You should also decide who can best help you with the various problems involved in a divorce. When a lawyer is billing you on an hourly rate, it is wise to use him or her for legal matters and to rely on friends, family, or professional counselors for your nonlegal, emotional, and supportive needs.

DO I HAVE TO HIRE A LAWYER?

The law states that a person may act as his or her own lawyer and may represent himself or herself in court. But since legal proceedings are quite specialized, complicated, and detailed, a person without legal training could have a difficult time with the technical procedures of the court. Most people do not know or understand the complexities of the law or comprehend all of the consequences of a legal proceeding. However, a person without an attorney can handle her own simple uncontested divorce.

To protect yourself, you should either be represented by an attorney or at least thoroughly discuss the matter with an attorney before proceeding on your own. This handbook makes every effort to be accurate and authoritative, but it cannot provide specific legal advice, nor can it be a substitute for an attorney.

WHAT ARE INJUNCTIONS AND TEMPORARY RESTRAINING ORDERS? HOW CAN THEY HELP ME?

An injunction is a court order telling a person to do or not to do some specific thing, such as move out of a house or stop using physical violence against you. A temporary restraining order is a kind of injunction or court order sometimes issued as part of a divorce action. A court may grant a temporary restraining order without letting the person it affects know about it until the order is officially delivered by the sheriff. A court will grant a temporary restraining order *only* when *immediate and irreparable* harm will be suffered unless the order is issued and served.

A temporary restraining order stays in effect for only ten days; and within those ten days, the court must have a hearing, or meeting, with you, your spouse, and your attorneys, if any, as to whether the temporary restraining order shall continue in effect. This hearing is usually called a ''hearing on an order to show cause,'' which requires the person being restrained to give reasons why the temporary restraining order should not be continued. At that hearing, the defendant has a chance to explain his or her side. The court is reluctant to take long-term action against anyone without letting them have a chance to tell their side of the story. If the temporary restraining order is continued in effect it is called a ''preliminary injunction.'' The same kinds of orders (to vacate the house, give up custody of the children, pay temporary support, etc.) are found in both temporary restraining orders and preliminary injunctions. A preliminary injunction is for the ''pendency'' of an action. When the decree is finally granted and the divorce is no longer ''pending,'' a permanent injunction will be granted, for example, ''The defendant is permanently enjoined and restrained from visiting the plaintiff's home or her place of employment, from striking, harassing, or harming her in any manner.'' The permanent injunction replaces the preliminary injunction.

A temporary restraining order should not be confused with a temporary order. A temporary restraining order is granted without notice when immediate and irreparable harm is threatened; it is served on your husband. A temporary order is usually granted after notice is given to your husband and after both sides have had a chance to be heard. It spells out temporary arrangements for child custody, support, who pays what bills, etc., while the divorce is pending.

Temporary orders are not always necessary but are often used when a married couple cannot agree on what should happen while the divorce is in progress. Often a husband will refuse to pay bills or support as a means of putting pressure on his wife during the negotiation process. A temporary order makes the arrangements formal and compulsory.

In a simple, uncontested divorce, there is usually no need for a temporary order.

WHAT HAPPENS IF A COURT ORDER IS IGNORED?

If your husband does not obey a temporary restraining order or other temporary or permanent order of the court, you must begin further legal proceedings to enforce the order. This means that another court hearing will be scheduled and your husband may be cited for contempt of court for failing to follow the court's order. The court may impose such sanctions as imprisonment for a set time, imprisonment until the order is complied with (for example, "Defendant shall be held in jail until he reveals the whereabouts of the child of the parties"), a fine, or a fine and/or a jail term suspended upon the party's good behavior.

Usually the police and the sheriff's department will not enforce a temporary restraining order or other court order. Only the court can enforce it, and then only after a hearing. A temporary restraining order or other court order will be effective in the long run when the court enforces it, but it might not provide the assistance and response that you need immediately.

Under the Utah Spouse Abuse Act you can obtain a temporary restraining order in a domestic matter without filing and pursuing a divorce. A temporary restraining order is a complaint that specifies the abuse or attempted abuse, your belief that the abuse will continue, the specific protection you want, and the specific permanent protection you want ordered at the hearing. Every county court clerk has the necessary forms. In most cases, you can fill out and file the papers the day you request them. Most people can fill out and file the papers without an attorney to assist them. If you live in Salt Lake County, the Legal Aid Society can assist you in filling out the papers. If you live elsewhere, the clerk of the court will assist you in preparing them.

WHAT IS A PERMANENT INJUNCTION?

A permanent injunction is a final court order included in a divorce decree which permanently orders a husband or wife to do or not to do something. For example, if your husband has harassed you at work or at home, a part of the divorce decree may "enjoin and restrain" him from such harassment. If this order is violated, he may be found in contempt of court and punished after a full court hearing such as those discussed above.

HOW DOES THE JUDGE DECIDE WHO GETS CUSTODY OF THE CHILDREN?

There are no set rules. The judge has the power under the statutes to award custody of children under the age of eighteen in a "just and proper" way. Other key phrases are "as may be equitable" and considering "the best interests of the child." The law says a judge should consider the best interests of each child and the past conduct and demonstrated moral standards of each parent.[10] A court will also ask who has been the child's primary care giver.

The law states that a judge may discuss with a child of any age his or her desires as to future custody, but that those expressed desires are not controlling. Prior statutes set an age limit of twelve (later lowered to ten) concerning the time a child might suggest a nonbinding preference to the court.

CAN I LOSE CUSTODY OF MY CHILD BECAUSE I'M A LESBIAN?

In child custody hearings, the primary consideration is the child's welfare. In determining the best interests of the child, a court must consider all relevant factors. In a 1980 case in which the wife was a lesbian, the Utah Supreme Court held that sexual preference in itself is not enough to deprive a parent of custody.[11] However, if the parent is exposing a child to, or requiring a child's participation in, any sexual activity prohibited by law or doing anything else the court decides is not in the best interest of the child, his or her custody or visitation rights may be restricted.

WHAT ABOUT JOINT CUSTODY?

Although a divorce decree may grant custody to one parent or the other, the parents, by informal agreement and without going back to court, can rearrange or change their custody/visitation program any way they choose. Most divorce decrees simply provide that "reasonable visitation" rights (see next section) be enjoyed by the noncustodial parent. The court does this so that the parties can work out visitation as necessary when their situations change. By the same token, the parties can, by informal agreement, make whatever custody or visitation arrangements they feel are best for themselves and their children.

Joint child custody is an option under Utah law which is becoming more common among divorcing parents. Joint custody means that the divorced parents share responsibility for the care, control, and custody of a child under eighteen. Joint custody can take several forms, all of which require the parents to outline a program compatible with their work schedules, living arrangements, finances, and the child's schooling. It can mean that the parents alternate custody every week, every month, or every six months. It can mean that one parent retains actual physical custody of the child but that both parents jointly make decisions about the child's daily needs and are jointly responsible for the child's well-being.

The court's ultimate goal in any divorce action involving children is to provide for the "best interests of the child." If those interests are best served by a joint custody arrangement of some type, a Utah court will allow such an arrangement. If the divorcing couple are not both willing to work together in the best interests of their child, there cannot be "joint custody" and one parent must be awarded sole custody. Either parent, if unwilling to cooperate, can prevent a joint custody agreement.

The dynamics of divorce often prevent joint custody from being a possible solution, although that seems to be changing as more parents who feel the need to divorce see the benefits of a continuing strong, healthy relationship between both mother and child and father and child.

If divorced parents can work together, joint custody arrangements can benefit children and minimize the harm that often occurs to them in divorce.

WHAT ARE REASONABLE VISITATION RIGHTS?

Normally in a divorce, one parent is awarded custody of the child or children and the other is given "reasonable visitation rights." "Reasonable visitation rights" means whatever the two parents agree upon. If they cannot agree on visiting schedules or arrangements, they can go back to court and have the judge designate exact times, places, and methods for visits.

The judge prefers that parents work out their own visitation schedules, allowing the person with visitation rights as much time as possible with the child without disrupting the family routine. The court will, however, establish a precise visiting schedule if necessary.

HOW DO THE NEW CHILD SUPPORT GUIDELINES WORK?

In every divorce in which dependent children are involved, the divorcing parties must each submit a child support worksheet. Different worksheets are available depending on whether you are seeking sole custody, joint custody, or split custody. Split custody means that you take some of the children and your husband takes the others. The amount of child support is based on each parent's income. The theory is that a child is entitled to enjoy both parents' standards of living. The amount you come up with on the worksheet is the amount the judge will presume to be an appropriate amount of child support. This means that the judge must order the noncustodial parent to pay that amount unless you or your husband can convince the judge that your situation is different enough that the amount should be higher or lower. The guidelines serve as an encouragement for most couples to agree on the issue of child support.

HOW LONG IS CHILD SUPPORT PAID?

In Utah, women and men are minors only until they are eighteen years old. A divorce decree usually stipulates that child support must be paid for minor children, and support normally stops at age eighteen or when a child leaves home and takes on the responsibilities of an adult. However, it is not unusual to find divorce decrees that provide for support to continue until a child completes high school or college. Child support may also be ordered past the ages of eighteen and twenty-one for handicapped or disabled children.

Minority can also be lost by marriage or by a determination (usually by the juvenile court) that the child is "emancipated."

A specific decree can spell out the duration of child support in each different situation, requiring it to be paid until the child is eighteen, twenty-one, or until the child is eighteen unless he or she remains a full-time student, in which case it may be required until the age of twenty-one.

AFTER THE DIVORCE, WHO CLAIMS THE CHILDREN AS DEPENDENTS FOR INCOME TAX PURPOSES?

After 1984, a parent who has custody of a child for the greater part of the year is treated as the parent who provides more than half the child's support and is thus allowed to claim the child as a dependent for federal income tax purposes.

After 1984, a divorced, *non*custodial parent may claim a child as a dependent for federal income tax purposes only if the custodial parent signs a written declaration to the effect that he or she will not claim the child and the noncustodial parent attaches this written declaration to his or her tax return; or a pre-1985 divorce decree gives the dependency exemption to the noncustodial parent and he or she provides at least $600 for the child's support during the year.

Child support is not taxable to the receiving party nor is it deductible to the paying party.

HOW ARE DEBTS AND PROPERTY DIVIDED IN UTAH?

There is no set standard for the division of debts and property in a divorce action. The judge has the power and the duty to make a "fair" division of the property acquired during the marriage.

Usually each of you can keep all the property you had before the marriage. The judge will usually decide that whoever has custody of the children needs more of the property to care adequately for them. If there is only one car, it usually goes to the person who needs it to go to and from work. Each of the parties will be awarded their own personal property, clothing, belongings, and effects.

In the same way, the standards for dividing the debts and obligations of the marriage is simply a "fair" division. The person best able to pay is usually responsible for the debts. The judge also considers who will benefit from the payment or who has benefited from whatever created that particular debt. This means that whoever is awarded the house will usually be required to make the mortgage payments and the person awarded the car or the furniture will probably have to pay the outstanding debts on them. Debts for items which benefited the entire family, such as food, utilities, clothing, and rent, will usually be the responsibility of the husband, since he is usually the one who has been the primary financial support of the family.

Personal effects are things like your toothbrush, wallet, driver's license, birth certificate, etc. Clearly, you and your husband should be able to divide those up without too much difficulty. You should also make your own division of small items of household property like pots and pans, cookbooks, etc. It is not a good use of your money to have two attorneys, each getting $75 per hour and using the expensive and cumbersome machinery of the legal system, to decide whether wife or husband gets the $2.98 Foley cake pan and the twelve pints of homemade chili sauce.

The court will resolve such disputes if you are unable to, but it is likely that no one will be completely satisfied. Making a compromise with your spouse on your own is much better than letting the court do it. Allowing the judge to decide gives up any control either of you might have had.

If you're disagreeing over something valuable and expensive—a store of fine wines, a valuable stamp or coin collection, a valuable work of art, antique furniture, an elaborate set of silver, etc.—the court will want to establish a value by appraisal, purchase price, or replacement price, and consider the value in dividing up the total assets of the parties.

After a divorce, people find that two households are more expensive than one—two rent payments, two phone bills, etc. The division of property and debts, plus child support, alimony, and legal expenses, usually means that both spouses must accept a lower standard of living than they had during the marriage.

It is important to remember that while the court can divide the debts between the two of you, your creditors can still pursue either one of you on any debt that the two of you incurred together, just as they can on any debt that was incurred for a family expense.

For example, even if the judge has ordered your husband to take over the bill to the furniture store, the furniture store can still choose to sue you alone or with your husband for the bill. If that occurs, you still have to defend yourself in court against the furniture company. If you do go to court, you cannot use as a defense the fact that your husband was ordered to pay the bill. If you or your husband owes the money, the company will probably get a judgment against you. You can sue your former husband for that bill, but you can't force the department store to choose to sue your husband instead of you.

WHAT IS ALIMONY?

Alimony is support money for a divorced spouse. Historically only women could receive alimony; now, by law in Utah and most states, a man can receive alimony, especially when he is "dependent," unable to support himself. "Alimony" is "spousal support."

Alimony is a continuation of the marital, moral, and legal obligation to support a spouse, especially a dependent spouse. Unless the divorce decree specifically provides otherwise, alimony automatically ends when the spouse receiving it remarries, because the law presumes that someone else now has the marital, moral, and legal obligation to provide support.

Alimony is nearly always granted to a wife who has remained at home, has raised several children during many years of marriage, has not worked outside the home, and has been totally dependent on her husband for financial support. Alimony will probably not be awarded in a marriage of short duration with no children or when both spouses work or have the ability to support themselves.

Alimony may also be granted for a short transitional period of time—a couple of years, for instance—so that the dependent spouse can finish school, acquire job skills, etc. If you are awarded transitional alimony, the court must have a specific reason for feeling that you will be able to support yourself when the transition period is over.

In cases where no alimony or only token alimony was awarded (e.g., $1 per year), you can go back to court to ask for alimony if your circumstances have changed substantially. For example, you could ask for money if your health changed to the point where you could not keep your job.

Under most circumstances, alimony is taxable as income to the receiving party and deductible to the paying party.

CAN MY HUSBAND REFUSE TO PAY ALIMONY BECAUSE I'M A LESBIAN?

No. The court orders alimony payments based on financial need, not sexual preference.

CAN I DATE BEFORE MY DIVORCE IS FINAL?

It usually takes three months for a divorce to become final. During that time the husband and wife are still legally married and cannot remarry; thus people pending divorce are *not* single people.

If you are still legally married to one person and date another person, it will probably cause friction between you and your husband. If you date while the divorce is pending, your husband may threaten to use that fact to prevent you from getting custody of any children involved. The court may consider this factor, but dating alone usually would not prevent you from being awarded custody.

Practically speaking, dating while a divorce is pending is not a problem in most cases.

WHAT DOES A DIVORCE DO TO MY WILL AND MY SPOUSE'S WILL?

By law, a divorce nullifies any provision of a will that devises, bequeaths, or gives the former spouse property. After a divorce, the parties should prepare new wills to prevent problems that may arise when portions of a will are invalidated.

8

PHYSICAL AND MENTAL HEALTH

PHYSICAL HEALTH

WHO CAN HELP PAY FOR MEDICAL CARE?

If you or a family member faces necessary medical treatment, you should first determine whether any insurance you or the family member has at work will help, and if so, the extent of the benefits. If you or your spouse is a veteran, there may be veterans' benefits available. If you suffer an injury in an accident or at your job, you may be eligible for benefits from another party's insurance or from workers' compensation. If you are injured because of a defective product, you may have a product liability claim, which could require the manufacturer or distributor to pay damages to you, including the costs of medical treatment.

Many elderly persons are eligible for Medicare, and Medicaid may be available to persons with limited financial means. Private charities and some hospitals offer help; charitable services to children are commonly offered at Utah hospitals. Do not be embarrassed about inquiring.

Few insurance plans or government programs will assist with strictly elective procedures, such as cosmetic surgery, unless the reason for the elective procedure is an injury or illness.

WHAT IS A MEDICAL MALPRACTICE CLAIM?

The law recognizes that neither physicians nor hospitals can guarantee the success of any procedure or treatment, but the law holds them liable if they are negligent in performing it. A medical practitioner must exercise that standard of care which is reasonable under the circumstances and which meets the prevailing standards within the particular area or field (e.g., surgery) in which the service, procedure, or treatment was done. A bad result does not necessarily justify a claim for malpractice.

WHAT IS INFORMED CONSENT?

Medical practitioners must inform their patients about the risks of procedures that are anticipated or that may be required; patients are asked to sign a release before they receive certain types of medical treatment. The release generally prevents the practitioner from facing liability for ordinary, foreseeable risks.

WHAT SHOULD I DO IF I THINK I HAVE A CLAIM?

If you believe that the medical care you or a family member received did not meet reasonable standards of care, consult with an attorney about the possibility of seeking damages. A number of attorneys handle medical malpractice actions on a contingent fee basis, which means they will accept as their fee for services a percentage of any settlement or award.

Learn exactly what a contingent fee agreement involves; many attorneys ask the client to pay out-of-pocket expenses. If these expenses include items like the fees to be charged by necessary expert witnesses, the out-of-pocket charges which you are agreeing to pay can be large.

The negligence you claim may be the responsibility of one or more physicians or members of a hospital staff. Ordinarily, nurses and technicians are employees of the hospital, so a suit against the hospital includes claims against its employees or agents. Sometimes there are several elements to the negligence, and several parties may be partially responsible under the law. Generally, they must all be named in a single proceeding, and you may settle with one or more of them at different times as the action progresses.

You may have a claim that procedures were performed without your informed consent. If you believe that you were not fully advised about possible consequences or about the procedures and their risks, consult with an attorney.

WHAT WILL HAPPEN?

In any medical malpractice action, you will need to release your medical and hospital records for review and evaluation so that it can be determined whether, in good medical and legal judgment, you have a claim that is worth pursuing. You may have to be examined by qualified medical practitioners.

In some cases, the attorney will engage in settlement discussions and will recommend whether to settle or go to trial. The decision is yours, but you should listen carefully to any advice and weigh the risks carefully; a jury or court may not make any award at all.

IS THERE A TIME LIMIT?

Medical malpractice claims must be brought promptly; the normal statute of limitations on such an action is two years from the event or occurrence. There are some circumstances in which the time limit may not start running, but do not count on extensions: consult with an attorney promptly.

Medical malpractice actions in Utah are referred to a screening panel with three or more members, including a medical practitioner, a lay citizen, and an attorney. Although the panel's view about the merits of the claim is not binding on the courts, its conclusion may indicate the way your claim will be perceived and may result in a settlement offer without further proceedings.

WHAT KIND OF AWARD CAN BE EXPECTED?

Settlements and jury awards in medical malpractice actions vary greatly. Very large awards make the newspapers, but the more ordinary settlements and judgments do not. A settlement or award may pay some or all of the costs of past and future medical care and treatment and may offer some compensation for pain and suffering. If the original costs of medical treatment have been paid by insurance or by a government agency, you may be required to reimburse the payor from your award. Have your attorney check on this as early as possible.

WHAT IS A STRUCTURED SETTLEMENT?

Some cases are settled with a ''structured settlement.'' A structured settlement works like an annuity or time payment and usually provides an initial lump sum payment, which may cover medical bills and current treatment, followed by periodic payments over time. These settlements may be very helpful, especially if you or the patient will require medical care or special assistance in the future. They may also have favorable tax and money management consequences.

SHALL I SETTLE?

If you have either a meritorious medical malpractice claim (which the physician's or hospital's attorney may recognize) or a very complex claim that may be expensive to defend, the defendants or their insurers may offer a settlement. Consider each settlement offer carefully with your attorney; some offers will be obviously inappropriate, but a small or inappropriate offer may open the door to further negotiations for something better. Settling an action before trial will probably reduce the amount of fee that you must pay to your attorney and will save you the effort of a trial. Settlement, like going to trial, is not an exact science, and risks and benefits should be examined.

If you are injured by a defective product or in an accident caused by others, you may receive an early offer of settlement from the insurer or the manufacturer. Be careful to understand the nature of any settlement offer before you agree to it; what seems generous now may prove inadequate in the future. It is wise to consult an attorney.

An attorney may also assist you in increasing a worker's compensation award or in obtaining coverage which an employer is seeking to deny. The attorney's fee for such a case is set by law and will be paid by the employer if the claim is successful.

WHAT ARE THE LAWS REGARDING BIRTH CONTROL? DO I NEED A PRESCRIPTION FOR BIRTH CONTROL DEVICES?

The pill, an IUD, and a diaphragm all require a doctor's prescription. Other methods, such as condoms or foam, are available without a prescription. A druggist can explain which ones are available. Prescription methods are usually long-term; one purpose of the law requiring a prescription is to be sure the patient understands possible side effects and how to use the method correctly.

MUST PARENTS KNOW OR CONSENT?

Generally, teenagers do not need their parents' consent to receive birth control services. However, Utah currently requires an unmarried minor to obtain the prior written consent of a parent or guardian to use any public funds (medical card, state or county health department services) to obtain contraceptives.

Women over eighteen or married currently face no restrictions in obtaining birth control services or contraceptives.

WHAT IS STERILIZATION?

Sterilization is a medical procedure intended to make it permanently impossible to have children. The usual methods for women are tubal ligation, hysterectomy, or the removal of ovaries. Men are made sterile by a generally irreversible method called vasectomy. No sterilization method should be permitted without a thorough understanding of the procedures and their consequences.

WHAT ARE THE LEGAL CONDITIONS FOR STERILIZATION?

State law provides that a woman and her partner may be sterilized by a physician if the person (1) is at least eighteen years old, (2) voluntarily consents, and (3) is capable of understanding the nature and consequences of sterilization and available alternate methods of contraception. A married person under eighteen, not living with or dependent upon parents, may be sterilized if the second two conditions are met.

The law provides special protection for people who want to be sterilized and who are institutionalized—meaning those who reside in a mental health facility, a residential facility for handicapped or disabled persons, a nursing home, or a foster home. The physician who performs the sterilization is responsible for examining the circumstances carefully and counseling the person to be sure there has been no coercion or improper influence by reason of the institutionalization.

CAN I BE STERILIZED WITHOUT MY CONSENT?

No one capable of giving informed consent can be forced to undergo sterilization. However, a person who is incapable of giving informed consent can be sterilized if a court orders sterilization, even if it is unwanted, under limited circumstances.

A parent, spouse, guardian, custodian, or other interested person may file a petition for a court order of sterilization. The court then appoints an attorney to represent the person and hears evidence. The court must consider the best interest of the person and what decision the person would make if capable of giving informed consent. It must then find proof beyond a reasonable doubt that the person will suffer serious physical or psychological injury if sterilization is not performed.

The law does not prohibit medical treatment for sound therapeutic reasons that incidentally involves the destruction of reproductive functions, such as treatment for cancer.

IS ABORTION LEGAL?

The United States Supreme Court has held that the fundamental right of privacy includes a woman's right to decide whether to terminate her pregnancy, but the right must be balanced against the state's interest in protecting both the potentiality of human life and the woman's health. Recent decisions indicate that states may impose some regulations on the process. Check with an attorney or an agency that gives family planning advice if questions arise or if new laws are announced, so that you can ascertain their impact on you.

The law currently recognizes three trimesters in pregnancy, with different considerations for each. During the first trimester, the woman's right to choose an abortion is paramount over the state's interests, and the state has little control over abortions. Currently, licensed physicians may perform first trimester abortions in their offices.

As the pregnancy progresses and the possibility of complications increases, the state may intervene to protect the woman's health. During the second trimester, Utah requires that abortions be performed in a state-certified hospital or clinic.

During the third trimester, when the fetus has a reasonable chance to survive outside the womb, a state may forbid an abortion except when necessary to save the life or health of the woman. Utah forbids abortions after the seventh month except when necessary to save the woman's life or to prevent serious and permanent damage to her health.

MUST A HUSBAND OR PARENTS BE NOTIFIED?

There is no minimum-age requirement for obtaining an abortion. However, Utah law requires the physician to notify the parents or guardian of an unemancipated minor, that is, a person under eighteen, but not if the person under eighteen is married or is not living with or dependent upon parents. Utah requires the physician to notify the husband, if possible; the appellate courts in Utah have not finally determined whether a putative father may have a right to prevent a nontherapeutic abortion at any stage of the pregnancy.

WILL MEDICAID PAY FOR AN ABORTION?

Medicaid will pay for abortion only in life-endangering pregnancies.

MENTAL HEALTH

WHAT IS MEANT BY "MENTAL HEALTH"?

Mental health is a broad term often defined as the absence of identifiable or significant mental disorder. A mentally healthy person feels comfortable about herself, interacts harmoniously with others, functions constructively in social and physical situations, and meets personal and societal needs without undue stress.

The community has an interest in protecting a person who has a psychiatric disorder that significantly impairs functioning and threatens the well-being of that person or others. If commitment is considered, legal procedures must be followed (see below). With constantly improving therapy, vocational guidance, and medical treatment, commitment may be unnecessary or inappropriate, and fear of possible commitment should not deter anyone from seeking help.

IS THERE HELP?

Mental health services cover a wide range of facilities and treatments for both mild and severe problems. More community-based services have become available in recent years, and increasing numbers of outpatient clinics, general hospital psychiatric units, and private psychiatric hospitals offer help. Some nursing homes care for the aged or chronic mental patient. Treatment ranges from intensive, for the acutely ill, to community-based aftercare programs. The individual's particular problem determines the services needed. The Utah Health Systems Agency recognizes three categories of mental health service:

1. *Crisis Intervention Services* focus on controlling and relieving disabilities so persons will not hurt themselves or others. These services include emergency intervention, medical treatment, and therapy.

2. *Rehabilitation Services* work with those in no immediate danger but unable to care for themselves fully. Services include occupational therapy, medication maintenance, recreation, vocational training, and self-care skills.

3. *Prevention Services* are designed to prevent future problems by helping persons acquire interpersonal and working skills so they are more successful as individuals, as part of a couple, in a family, and at work.

WHERE CAN I GET HELP?

The Utah Health Systems Agency lists the types of publicly funded and private facilities that offer treatment.

Psychiatric hospitals: Public or private hospitals primarily devoted to inpatient psychiatric care for the mentally ill.

General hospitals with a psychiatric unit: General, acute-care hospitals that provide psychiatric care, usually for a short term, in a special unit. Most general hospitals accept psychiatric patients for short-term crisis care.

Mental health centers: Comprehensive Mental Health Centers (CMHCs) set up by federal law to provide a comprehensive array of services, usually under a federal, state, and local partnership. Their services include community-based inpatient, partial outpatient, and emergency care; consultation and education; transitional care or residential treatment; special services for children, the aged, and for alcohol and drug abusers; and screening and follow-up care for institutionalized patients.

Residential treatment centers: Structured twenty-four-hour care facilities that provide treatment to those clinically diagnosed as mentally or emotionally disabled. They provide residential and other assistance in daily activities but do not always offer licensed professional nursing services.

Long-term care facilities: Residential facilities offering nursing care to mentally ill patients. These facilities may be categorized by the intermediate or skilled level of nursing care they offer.

Day treatment services: Partial care providers with planned therapeutic programs for people who can benefit from greater care than is available in an outpatient clinic setting but who do not need twenty-four-hour care. Day/Evening Care and Sheltered Workshops are examples; they offer supervision in an independent and transitional living arrangement.

Private practitioner: Private practitioners provide care to a wide range of clients who are both publicly and privately financed. Practitioners include psychiatrists, psychologists, psychiatric social workers, psychiatric nurses, marriage and family counselors, educational counselors, and other specially trained and licensed practitioners.

To find these facilities and practitioners, check the telephone directory under "hospital," "mental health," and "counselors."

HOW MUCH WILL IT COST?

Mental health care costs vary widely according to patient needs and treatment setting. Hospitalization generally costs more than outpatient therapy; private facilities generally cost more than public ones. Although all mental health programs charge for their services, you may be eligible for reduced rates through your local CMHC. State law prohibits refusing services because of inability to pay. If hospitalization is required, the state can collect money from Medicaid or from available Social Security disability benefits to help pay for care.

It is your right as a mental health care consumer to ask for and receive information about costs of treatment, methods of payment, and medical assistance funding programs for which you may qualify.

WHAT IF HOSPITALIZATION IS RECOMMENDED?

If a mental health professional determines that hospitalization is required, you may be admitted to a local hospital with psychiatric beds or to the Utah State Hospital in Provo, which functions under the Division of Mental Health in the Utah State Department of Social Services. The State Hospital provides services to individuals with chronic problems so severe that few or no community-based entities can provide adequate help. Some persons referred to the State Hospital are too dangerous or difficult to manage elsewhere. Children under sixteen may be admitted to the State Hospital if a parent or legal guardian applies in their behalf.

WHAT IF A PATIENT IS TOO SICK TO DECIDE?

If a patient is too sick to choose treatment, then someone else may take the patient to a mental health facility or hospital. The staff will decide what level of care is necessary and whether to admit. If a mental health professional determines that a patient is too disoriented to be responsible for health and safety, the staff may arrange for an "involuntary admission." The difference between voluntary and involuntary admission is that those voluntarily admitted may leave at any time, unless clinical personnel have decided the patient might harm herself or others or unless legal involuntary hospitalization proceedings have been started.

HOW DOES INVOLUNTARY COMMITMENT HAPPEN?

County mental health programs can hospitalize mental patients involuntarily by court order under Utah laws.

A responsible person who knows the circumstances and believes the patient to be mentally ill and in need of involuntary hospitalization must apply to the court in writing. A "responsible person" is usually a relative who has assumed responsibility for the patient's care. The application must be accompanied by a certificate from a licensed physician or a state-designated examiner stating that he or she has examined the patient within the last seven days, believes the patient is mentally ill, and recommends involuntary hospitalization. Alternatively, the responsible person must include a written statement that the patient has refused to submit to an examination by a physician or examiner.

The court will order an examination, but the patient is entitled to a hearing and may be represented by a lawyer. After the hearing, the judge will order hospitalization only if all of the following questions are answered in the affirmative:

Does the patient have a mental illness?

Because of this illness, does the patient pose an "immediate danger of physical injury" to self or others? "Immediate danger" may be inability to feed herself or a dependent child, to stay on the sidewalk instead of blundering into traffic because of disorientation, or being unable to perform other normal and necessary functions.

Does the patient lack the ability to carry out a rational decision-making process about treatment for mental illness?

Are there no less restrictive but equally appropriate alternatives to court-ordered hospitalization?

Will the hospital or mental health facility provide appropriate and adequate treatment?

If the questions cannot all be answered yes, the court will dismiss the proceeding, and the patient cannot be kept involuntarily in any mental health facility, but the patient may agree at any time to become a voluntary patient.

If the court does place the patient, it may designate the facility; such placements are frequently made with the State Hospital for either a temporary (less than six months) or an indeterminate period. County mental health programs track court-placed patients and their treatment plan in conjunction with the State Division of Mental Health.

WHAT LEGAL RIGHTS DO I HAVE AFTER ADMISSION?

Admission to a facility for mental health care does not mean a patient cannot make legal decisions. Unless the court finds the patient incapacitated, the patient can exercise all civil rights, including the right to dispose of property, enter into contracts, make purchases, make a will, vote, marry, and (health permitting) drive a car.

WHAT IS "INCAPACITATION"?

An "incapacitated person" is anyone who is impaired by reason of mental illness or deficiency, physical illness or disability, advanced age, chronic drug use or intoxication, or other causes (except youth) to the extent that the person lacks sufficient understanding or capacity to make or communicate responsible decisions about personal well-being.

The allegedly incapacitated person or anyone interested in that person's welfare may ask the court for a finding of "incapacitation" and the appointment of a guardian to provide care. If appointed, the guardian then determines where the person lives, provides for the person's care and comfort, cares for the person's personal possessions, and gives consent for medical treatment when necessary.

A finding of incapacitation and the appointment of a guardian does *not* mean the person is mentally ill or can be involuntarily hospitalized. However, if a person has been found mentally ill and has been involuntarily hospitalized, it may not be necessary to have additional court proceedings to appoint a guardian.

If the incapacitated person cannot manage his or her property and financial affairs, someone may petition the court to appoint a conservator who is granted legal power to manage only the property and funds of the incapacitated person for the person's benefit. A guardian has greater responsibility for personal care and well-being.

The incapacitated person or any other interested person may petition the court at any time to end either a guardianship or a conservatorship.

WHAT WILL HAPPEN IN THE HOSPITAL?

State law provides that every patient is entitled to humane care and to medical care that meets the prevailing standards of medical, psychiatric, nursing, social work, and clinical psychology practice. Staff members will develop a mental health treatment plan for the patient.

If you are hospitalized, ask questions about medications and treatment methods when you see a therapist or doctor. Try to work out any problems with medication or therapy with the staff. A patient has the right to refuse medication and to stop seeing a therapist. If a voluntary patient refuses all medicine and treatment, the hospital may discharge the patient because help is being refused.

Every patient has the right to communicate by sealed mail or otherwise with persons inside or outside the hospital and to receive visitors. Patients cannot be subjected to unnecessary mechanical restraint or medication.

WILL MY THERAPIST TELL WHAT I SAY OR DO?

All health care professionals have ethical standards and rules of law that require holding patient information in strict confidence. Therapists will not reveal secrets or confidences to spouses, parents, children, or others. No one other than those treating a patient can see medical records without the patient's written consent. Legal penalties can be imposed against health care personnel and facilities for violating confidentiality requirements.

9

SOCIAL WELFARE LAWS

9

WHAT ARE UTAH'S BASIC SOCIAL WELFARE PROGRAMS?

The federal Social Security Act of 1935 established several programs designed to guarantee a minimum level of economic benefits for everyone. Today these programs include Social Security, a system of basic income security for most retired and disabled workers and their dependents, and for survivors of deceased workers (RSHDI); hospital and medical insurance for the aged and disabled (Medicare); health care and services for low income persons (Medicaid); benefits for those—usually coal miners—suffering from black lung; supplemental security income for people sixty-five or older, blind, or disabled (SSI); unemployment insurance; and general public assistance and welfare services.

While these programs are designed for all citizens, certain aspects may be particularly relevant to working women, working wives or mothers, and homemakers.

The actual dollar amounts and other requirements may change from year to year, but you can contact one of these agencies to determine the current status of a provision: Utah Legal Services (328-8891), Utahns Against Hunger (328-2561), or Utah Issues (521-2035).

WHAT ABOUT SOCIAL SECURITY?

Retirement, Survivors, Disability, and Health Insurance is a federally funded retirement insurance program for American workers.[1] Commonly called "Social Security," it is a government-administered insurance fund into which employees pay during their working years and from which they collect benefits when they retire or become disabled. It provides monthly cash benefits as a substitute for earned income to workers who are retired or totally disabled, to their dependents, and, after they die, to their surviving dependents.

Because the amount of monthly benefits you receive is based on your average earnings, you should be sure that each of your employers has your correct Social Security number and accurately reports your wages and the amount being withheld to the Social Security Administration. Before you are entitled to monthly benefits you must work for a certain amount of time, which is figured in three-month periods, or quarters. The amount of work time necessary for monthly benefits depends on the year in which you reach age sixty-two or the date of your death or disability or your spouse's death or disability.[2] Generally, a worker with fewer than six quarters (that is, one and one-half years or eighteen months) of employment will not qualify for regular old-age benefits. No one needs more than ten years of work to be eligible for benefits.

IF I WORK OUTSIDE MY HOME, WILL MY FAMILY AND I RECEIVE SOCIAL SECURITY BENEFITS?

As a working woman, you earn Social Security protection not only for yourself but also for your dependents. Even if you have no dependents, the Social Security credit you earn while you work is applied toward monthly benefits for the family you may have in the future.

WHEN CAN I RETIRE AND RECEIVE BENEFITS?

If you have worked the necessary number of quarters, you can retire as early as age sixty-two, but you will have to accept reduced benefits. Payments to people who retire before age sixty-five are permanently reduced to balance the longer period of time they will be receiving checks. The reduction formula—5/9 of 1 percent reduction for each month between the sixty-second and sixty-fifth birthdays—is applied against the worker's benefits.[3] This means that if you retire at sixty-two, your monthly benefits would be 20 percent less than the monthly amount you would receive if you retire at sixty-five and you have worked the necessary number of quarters. Similarly, if you retire after age sixty-five, the amount you receive will increase by 3 percent per year.[4]

IF I AM MARRIED, AM I ENTITLED TO MY HUSBAND'S BENEFITS IN ADDITION TO THOSE EARNED FROM MY OWN WORK RECORD?

No. If you are married, you can get retirement payments *either* on your own record *or* on your husband's, whichever will pay the larger benefits.[5] If you have worked all your adult life and have had high earnings, it is likely that your own benefits will be higher than those you could receive from your husband's work record. At sixty-five, a wife gets 50 percent of what her husband is entitled to at sixty-five or reduced benefits if she retires at sixty-two. But if you stopped working for several years or had lower earnings, your husband's payment might be higher than your own. When you apply for retirement benefits, the Social Security office should tell you whether your own record or your husband's will pay a higher amount. 9

In the same way, your husband can get retirement benefits on your record once he is sixty-two if he does not have a record which will pay him more.

WHAT HAPPENS IF I'M DISABLED?

If you become disabled and cannot work for a year or more, you can receive disability benefits.[6] "Disability" is a medical question that must be decided by at least one doctor. There is a Social Security Review Board which scrutinizes medical findings on disability, and it can accept or reject a doctor's recommendation. Disability standards are hard to meet, and the current trend is to make them even stricter. HHS (Health and Human Services), which oversees this program, has established a set of regulations that define "disability." "Disability" is thus a legal term, and an assertion by a doctor that you are disabled from performing any work will carry no weight unless accompanied by the objective tests that he relied upon in making this determination.

There is a five-step sequential evaluation Social Security must follow in determining disability.

1. *Are you currently working?* The work must meet criteria that determine it to be both substantial—it involves significant work activities, and gainful—it meets certain standards concerning how much is earned per month. If the answer is yes the evaluation stops at this point and you are judged not to be disabled.

2. *Do you suffer from a "severe" impairment?* This means that, based on medical evidence alone, you can show that your impairment significantly limits your physical or mental ability to do basic work activities. As with the first step, you are obligated to prove this.

3. *Does your impairment "meet or equal a listed impairment"?* At this stage you may show that based on medical evidence alone you are disabled. The regulations require that this determination be made on specific tests which usually produce numerical data. These standards are very difficult to meet, but if your impairment does meet or equal a listed impairment, the analysis proceeds to the next step.

4. *Can you do your past relevant work?* At this stage you must show that your impairments prevent you from performing every significant job (usually for three months or longer) that you have held for the past fifteen years. At this stage, vocational evidence regarding the requirements of your past work becomes relevant. If you can show that you can no longer perform your past work, the analysis proceeds to the next step.

5. *Is there any work existing in significant numbers in the national economy which you can perform?* At this stage the burden of proof shifts to the Social Security Administration, and they will often call a vocational expert to testify. If there is an insignificant number of such potential jobs you will be ruled "disabled." Whether or not you could actually be hired for any of these jobs is irrelevant. Here your age, education, and skills gained from work experience are taken into account, as well as the functional limitations resulting from your impairment and the functional requirements of proposed jobs. For example, a worker who is fifty-five or over is presumed "disabled" if she or he has less than a high school education, has worked in only semiskilled jobs, and has an impairment so severe that she or he can do only sedentary work (work sitting down). If the same worker is between eighteen and

forty-four, however, he or she is considered to be "retrainable" rather than disabled.

There is a five-month waiting period before you begin receiving disability benefits. Payments begin with the sixth full month of your disability and continue until you reach retirement age and begin to receive retirement benefits. If you have been eligible for disability payments for two consecutive years, you will also have Medicare coverage. If you are disabled, your children (including your stepchildren or legally adopted children) can also receive benefits based on your disability. Monthly benefits based on your disability are payable to your unmarried children under eighteen and to any of your children who become disabled themselves before age twenty-two and remain disabled. If you are getting disability benefits, your husband also qualifies for payment if he is sixty-two or older.

If the Review Board says you are disabled, you may be referred to vocational rehabilitation service counselors who will evaluate your ability to work, provide job training, and help you in job placement. As soon as you can work, you are no longer eligible for disability benefits.

WILL MY FAMILY RECEIVE SOCIAL SECURITY BENEFITS IF I DIE?

Both your spouse and your children can get monthly survivors' benefits if you die. Your family may be entitled to survivors' benefits even if you have only one and one-half years of work in the three years before you die. There is a lump-sum death payment of $255 to help pay funeral expenses. To be eligible for this payment you must be either a surviving spouse who was living with the deceased at the time of his or her death or separated only due to illness, or a dependent child. If your husband has no young children in his care at the time of your death, he must be sixty or older, or between fifty and sixty and disabled, to qualify for survivors' benefits on your work record. Your spouse will be entitled to benefits regardless of his age, if you are insured, if he has not remarried, and if he has in his care an unmarried child under eighteen or an older child who was disabled before the age of twenty-two.[7]

If the father of the children dies, Social Security will not require a showing that the child was dependent on the father at the time of death if the child is legitimate. If the child is illegitimate Social Security requires either proof of the child's dependency at the time of the father's death or substantial proof that the deceased is the father, which is often difficult to obtain. In spite of the potential unfairness of such regulations, the U.S. Supreme Court has held them to be constitutional. A child may also be entitled to disability benefits under the Supplemental Security Income program or based on his parent's earnings, though, like widow's benefits, this standard is more difficult to meet than ordinary disability determinations. During the 1989–90 term, the U.S. Supreme Court will consider for the first time whether this stricter standard is justifiable.

WHAT IF I INTERRUPT MY CAREER?

You need credit for a minimum amount of work to qualify for any Social Security benefits. If you stop working before you earn enough quarters of coverage, no benefits will be payable.[8] However, credits you earn will remain on your work record, and you can go back to work and earn the additional credits you need to qualify. This rule is particularly significant to you as a woman, since you may prefer to interrupt your career to stay home and raise children.

You should realize, however, that the *amount* of your monthly payments will be affected because you earned no income during the years you chose to remain at home. Your benefits may be somewhat lower since the amount of your payment is based on your average earnings over a period of years.[9] The years in which you had no or low income will lower the average. In addition, an interruption in your work history *may* make you ineligible for disability benefits. To qualify for disability benefits, you must have worked one-half of the time during the ten years before the disability occurred.[10]

AM I ELIGIBLE FOR SOCIAL SECURITY IF I WORK IN MY OWN OR SOMEONE ELSE'S HOME?

In most jobs, Social Security contributions are deducted from your pay automatically. But this may not be the case if you are a household worker, such as babysitters, maids, cooks, laundry workers, butlers, gardeners, chauffeurs, and people who do housecleaning or repair work.

If you are a household worker and your employer reports your earnings to Social Security, you can get one quarter of Social Security coverage for every $260 you earn. You should, therefore, show your employer your Social Security card and tell her or him to deduct Social Security contributions from your wages. If you fail to do so, you will not get Social Security credit for your work; and if you do not have enough credits, you and your family won't be entitled to monthly benefits based on your work record. However, you may still be entitled to the other types of benefits and assistance discussed in the rest of this chapter.

WHAT IF I EMPLOY A HOUSEHOLD WORKER?

If you employ a household worker, it is your responsibility to see that the wages you pay are properly reported. As an employer, you must deduct Social Security contributions from the wages, pay from your own pocket an amount equal to what you have deducted, and send the money to the Internal Revenue Service with a report of total wages paid. The report form and instructions are available at any IRS office.

WHAT IF I CHANGE MY NAME?

You should be sure that your Social Security record shows your correct name, particularly if you are employed, because your employer reports your earnings under the name you give her or him.

Whenever you change the name you use in employment, whether because of marriage, divorce, or any other reason, you should report the change to Social Security.[11] If you choose to continue using your maiden name after marriage, you do not have to report your marriage; just be certain you use your maiden name consistently throughout your employment.

Even if you do not work, you should report any name change so that your record will show the correct name when you apply for benefits. To report a name change, simply fill out a "Request for Change in Social Security Records." You can get this form at any Social Security office.

IF I'VE NEVER BEEN EMPLOYED CAN I RECEIVE BENEFITS BASED ON MY HUSBAND'S RECORD?

If you are a married woman and have never been employed, you are entitled to benefits based on your husband's work record when he becomes disabled or retires if you are caring for a child under eighteen or a disabled child who is entitled to benefits, regardless of your age, or if you do not have a child in your care but are sixty-two or older.[12] You are entitled to full wife's retirement benefits, or 50 percent of the amount your husband is entitled to, if you wait until sixty-five to collect these benefits.[13] If you get benefits before age sixty-five, the payment is permanently reduced.

If you are a widow who has never been employed, you can receive monthly survivor's benefits and your children may also be entitled to survivors' benefits. You can get a widow's benefit at any age if you are caring for a child who is under eighteen or disabled and entitled to benefits. These benefits will stop when you no longer have in your care a child who is under eighteen or disabled. If you are sixty or older when your husband dies, you are entitled to widow's benefits, even if you have no dependent children. If you are fifty and disabled, you are also eligible for these benefits.[14] If you are sixty-five or older at the time of your husband's death, you will receive the full amount of payments your husband would have received if he had lived.

If you are collecting benefits on behalf of your deceased husband and you remarry, and if you are *under* sixty, your payments based on his record will stop. You may become re-entitled to these payments if your subsequent marriage ends.[15] If you are *over* sixty, your payments could continue; but if your new husband gets Social Security checks, you have the option of taking a wife's benefit on his record if it would be larger than your widow's payment.

IF I GET DIVORCED, WILL I BE ENTITLED TO BENEFITS BASED ON MY EX-HUSBAND'S EARNINGS?

You are entitled to benefits when your ex-husband starts collecting retirement or disability payments if you are sixty-two or older and were married to him for at least ten years.

You may also get payments if your ex-husband dies, provided you are sixty or older (fifty, if you are disabled) and you were either married for at least ten years or have young children entitled to benefits on his record.

DOES SOCIAL SECURITY DISCRIMINATE AGAINST ME AS A WOMAN?

Social Security legislation has increasingly been attacked for discriminating on the basis of sex. Although this discrimination results in inequities which can affect both men and women, the inequities in fact fall primarily on women. This is largely because Social Security legislation was enacted at a time when women were assumed to be financially dependent on their husbands and marriage was assumed to be a lifetime arrangement. Today, half of all marriages break up and half of all married women work, yet Social Security legislation remains substantially the same as when it was enacted forty years ago.

An example of discrimination against women under present laws is illustrated by the fact that a person can claim benefits both as a wage earner and as a dependent, yet Social Security is structured so that any person, male or female, cannot get both a full benefit as a wage earner and a full benefit as a non-earning dependent. This may result in a two-income family paying more Social Security taxes on their combined wages, yet receiving fewer overall benefits than a couple with only one wage earner but the same income. Unless a wage-earning wife is entitled to more than half of her husband's primary benefit amount in her own right, she will not receive any additional benefits as a result of her own Social Security earnings and contribution. Although more women are active in the labor force, large numbers of women do not receive significant benefits from their contributions.

Further discrimination against women as a consequence of Social Security law is apparent in the current practice of averaging earnings to determine benefit amounts. Social Security benefits are based on the worker's average earnings in a specified number of years. Because of this, inflation and typical salary increases throughout a career can combine to create a situation in which the average salary is significantly smaller than the pre-retirement salary. Although this problem exists for both men and women, the consequences for women are much greater, partly because of employment discrimination. In addition, women often spend a period of time bearing and raising children, when they may earn very little or nothing. Women who work part-time or part of a year will also have low annual earnings. A pattern of absences from the labor force seriously affects a woman's right to disability benefits. Since the law does not currently view housework and homemaking as a valid occupation, a woman who spends years of her life in such labor may end up with little or no security in her old age. And, under current legislation, when a marriage lasts less than ten years, a divorced homemaker receives *no* Social Security benefits.

This discrimination has been considered by the Department of Health, Education, and Welfare. The Department has offered two proposals. One is a ''shared earnings'' approach, where family earnings would be pooled and each partner would be credited with half the total in computing benefits. The other is a ''two-tier'' approach, where a basic monthly benefit of $122 would be provided to each spouse over sixty-five, with an additional sum based on individual earnings. Either approach would ease many of the inequities found in the current system.

WHERE CAN I GET MORE INFORMATION?

If you would like to learn more about Social Security or to get a statement of your contributions to date, you can write to the Social Security Administration, 6401 Security Boulevard, Baltimore, Maryland 21235.

Be sure to include your Social Security number and birth date for identification. If you want to apply for benefits or need additional information, you can call your local Social Security office, which is listed under Social Security Administration in your telephone book.

WHAT IS SUPPLEMENTAL SECURITY INCOME (SSI)?

SSI is a federal cash benefit program that pays monthly benefits to people in financial need who are sixty-five or older and to blind or disabled people of any age who are in need.[16]

The aim of the program is to provide a basic cash income to people who have either no income or only a very small one. The amount of SSI payments you receive depends on your income and the value of any assets such as property you may own. Income you receive from Social Security, veterans' compensation, pensions, and gifts generally reduces the amount of your SSI payment.[17]

In 1989, the amount an individual could receive each month was $372.00. As of 1988 a couple could receive up to $504.00. When you apply for SSI benefits, the amount of income you receive from other sources is computed and, if it is below these levels, you will receive an additional check each month from SSI to bring your income up to the SSI benefit level. There is also a state supplement of $6, which the Utah Department of Social Services has recommended eliminating.

To be eligible for SSI you must be in financial need and be over sixty-five; or blind (with vision no better than 20/200 even with glasses, or "tunnel vision," or limited visual field of 20 degrees or less); or "disabled," which means you cannot engage in substantial gainful work because of a physical or mental impairment which has lasted, or is expected to last, twelve months or which can be expected to result in death.

SSI recipients are almost always eligible for food stamps and Medicaid, but you must apply for them separately. Because SSI is administered by the Social Security Administration, you should contact that agency to apply or to ask questions.

WHAT IS MEDICARE?

Contributions made to Social Security also fund Medicare. Medicare eligibility is based on your Social Security coverage and work history; you do not have to be in a low-income bracket to receive it. You are eligible for Medicare if you are sixty-five and are eligible for Social Security or Railroad Retirement benefits either as a retired worker or as the spouse or widow of a retired worker; or if you are disabled and have been receiving disability benefits for twenty-four months; or if you have end-stage renal disease and have required dialysis or a kidney transplant.[18]

Medicare has two parts: Part A, or hospital insurance, covers the cost of hospitalization, "extended care" provided by a hospital when you are not hospitalized, and home health care agencies. You automatically get hospital insurance if you qualify for Social Security benefits. If you don't have enough quarters of coverage to qualify, you can purchase the insurance for a yearly premium that changes each year.

Part B, medical insurance, covers medical and other health services, including a doctor's care. When you buy Part A, hospital insurance, the Part B medical insurance is optional and the price varies from year to year. The amount will be deducted from your Social Security check. You can sign up for Part B only during a "general enrollment period," each year from January 1 to March 31. There is a penalty of 10 percent of the premium for each year over sixty-five if you have delayed enrollment.

It is a good idea to apply for your Medicare insurance three months before the month in which you turn sixty-five. That means your coverage will begin the month of your birthday. Otherwise, there may be some delay. You can also apply during the three months after your sixty-fifth birthday. When you apply for Part A, hospital insurance, you will be automatically enrolled for Part B, medical insurance, unless you tell the Social Security office you do not want it.

For more information on Medicare and the exact services Parts A and B cover, call or write your local Social Security office. The telephone number is listed under the Social Security Administration in your local telephone book.

WHAT IS MEDICAID?

Medicaid is a federal- and state-funded program run by the state, which provides medical insurance for people with low incomes.[19] Eligible persons receive a card that they can present to doctors, druggists, hospitals, and other health care providers. Bills for medical services to card holders are sent to the state for payment, following a specific schedule of fees.

You are eligible for Medicaid if you receive SSI (see earlier section) or AFDC (see following section), but you must make separate application for it. You may also qualify if you are "medically needy," a term that means your income and resources are insufficient, in comparison with a standard set by the state, to pay for your medical care. If you are medically needy, you are responsible for your medical bills equal to the amount your income is above the Medicaid eligibility point (you must "spend down" to get coverage). Medicaid will pay the rest of your medical bills. In Utah, many elderly people as well as low-income families qualify for Medicaid through a medically needy status. Currently Utah is in violation of federal law in not counting medical bills already incurred in determining the amount you must pay to get coverage. State officials assert that they will drop the program rather than adhere to federal regulations.

Medicaid now provides many services in Utah, but because each state can limit the type of service provided, there are frequent changes in Medicaid services. Currently covered Medicaid services include hospital care, outpatient service like X-rays and laboratory services, doctors' fees, nursing home care, transportation for medical services (which must be authorized in advance except in emergencies), prescription drugs, some dental services, eye examinations and glasses, and sterilizations and abortions in limited circumstances.

WHAT IS AID TO FAMILIES WITH DEPENDENT CHILDREN (AFDC)?

Aid to Families with Dependent Children (AFDC) is a cooperative federal-state program that provides financial assistance to needy families. It is administered by the Utah Department of Social Services. The most common AFDC household consists of a single-parent family. The basic eligibility requirement for AFDC is that a household must include at least one ''eligible'' child or pregnant woman. An eligible child is one who is under eighteen years of age (or eighteen and completing high school), and who is deprived of the support or care of one parent because that parent is absent, deceased, or incapacitated. That eligible child must live with a parent or relative. Two-parent households can receive AFDC if one of the parents is ''incapacitated'' and therefore unable to support or care for the child.

People who apply for AFDC must assign their rights to child support to the State of Utah and must agree to assist the state in establishing paternity and collecting support. When the state collects child support from the absent parent, it reimburses itself for assistance provided to the family, and gives $50 of the monthly support collected to the AFDC family.

AFDC applicants and recipients must meet income and resource requirements in order to qualify for benefits. The amount of the monthly AFDC grant depends on the amount of income received by the household. Certain types of income are not counted when determining the AFDC grant. Exempt income includes food stamps, home produce, SSI income, cash gifts up to $30 in a three-month period, loans, and the first $50 in child support collected by the state.

AFDC applicants and recipients may own property and still receive assistance. The asset limit is $1,000. Certain resources and assets are exempt, such as the home and its contents, the value of the lot, water rights, and the first $1,500 equity in one car.

Persons who qualify for AFDC will almost always qualify for Medicaid health coverage as well as food stamps. Applications for AFDC are processed at the local Office of Community Operations, Department of Social Services.

WHAT ARE FOOD STAMPS?

Food stamps are government coupons that people can spend on food at regular grocery stores. People who are over sixty-five years of age can receive a check instead of coupons. Like other public benefits programs, eligibility for food stamps is based on income and resources. Almost anyone who is low-income is eligible for food stamps, including the disabled, elderly, some students, homeless people, and most legal aliens.

The resource limit for households is $2,000. If one of the household members is sixty or older, then the resource limit is $3,000. Resources include cash on hand, bank accounts, cars, land, and buildings. The household's home is not counted against the household's resource limit. The household's income affects the amount of food stamps that may be issued. The actual "countable" income is the amount less certain deductions like rent or utilities.

People who have very few resources and very low incomes can qualify for "expedited food stamps" and can receive their coupons within five days. Expedited food stamps are available to people who (1) have less than $100 cash and less than $150 gross monthly income; or (2) have a combined gross income and resources of less than a month's rent or mortgage payment; or (3) belong to a household in which all members are homeless; or (4) are migrant workers who are between jobs and won't receive more than $25 from the new job for at least ten days.

Applications for food stamps are processed at the local Department of Social Services, Office of Community Operations. Persons who apply should be prepared to verify their household composition, resources, and income.

IF I AM OUT OF WORK, CAN I COLLECT UNEMPLOYMENT COMPENSATION?

The unemployment insurance program provides temporary financial help to workers who meet certain requirements and who are out of work through no ''fault'' of their own.[20] ''Fault'' is a legal term which is frequently argued. Basically it means that you weren't fired with ''just cause'' or that you didn't quit without ''good cause.'' Sexual harassment on the job is recognized in Utah as ''good cause,'' and a woman who quits her job because of such harassment is entitled to unemployment.

The Utah Department of Employment Security, commonly known as Job Service, manages the program, and all claims or inquiries should be filed through that office. There are local offices in most counties.

Unemployment insurance payments are paid by employer and employee contributions.

You are eligible for such payments if you have been working at a job and federal payroll tax has been deducted from your pay check for at least twenty-six weeks. If you are eligible, the size of your payments and the length of time you can receive them depends on how long you worked and how much you earned.[21] Basically, to be eligible in Utah, you must fulfill the prior earnings requirement, have twenty-six weeks of deductions, and not be unemployed because of a labor dispute in which you, or a class of workers to which you belong, have participated, financed, or taken a direct interest. You must not be receiving other unemployment compensation or be on a bona fide vacation. You must also register to work at the local Job Service office when you file your claim and continue to report there at least once a week. You must be able to work and be available to work. That means you must look for a job and not impose unreasonable conditions on a future job.

WILL I GET UNEMPLOYMENT BENEFITS IF I STOP WORKING BECAUSE I AM PREGNANT?

Although there are no specific provisions in the Utah Employment Compensation Law about pregnancy, it is possible that pregnant women will face additional problems in meeting eligibility requirements.

The law requires that a person asking for these benefits be ''able'' to work. Your pregnancy will eventually interfere with your ability to work, at least for some period of time. Recently the United States Supreme Court ruled that an individual's ability to work had to be determined on a case-by-case basis, and that the state could not expect inability to work simply because of a pregnancy.[22]

If you decide to leave your job because you are pregnant, but you are still physically able to work, you may be entitled to unemployment compensation if you can prove that you are, in fact, still able to work. The fact that you have left your job on your own will also be considered, but that does not automatically mean you are ineligible. If you have taken maternity leave because you are no longer physically able to work, you cannot receive unemployment benefits since everyone receiving unemployment must be currently able to work and available for work. If you have any problems as a pregnant woman seeking unemployment benefits, you should contact an attorney or a legal aid society.

WILL I BE PAID WORKER'S COMPENSATION IF I AM INJURED ON THE JOB?

If you are injured because of an accident that happened while you were actually working, or if you are suffering from an ''occupational disease'' caused by the type of work you perform, you can receive money under the Utah Worker's Compensation Act.[23]

If you believe you have such an injury or disease, you should give your employer written notice as soon as possible, within at least forty-eight hours of the injury. You must also file a claim with the state Industrial Commission within three years of the accident, or the week in which you last received compensation payments, to be eligible for compensation.

WHAT CAN I DO IF I THINK I AM BEING TREATED UNFAIRLY BY ANY OF THESE AGENCIES?

It is always possible that an agency office has made a mistake regarding a claim you have made. If you feel the agency has discriminated against you, did not process your claim correctly, improperly stopped your benefits, or failed to give you the benefits you legally deserve, you should insist on an explanation. If you still do not agree with the decision of the agency, you should immediately contact an attorney or Utah Legal Services, file a written complaint with your local office, and request a fair hearing. At the hearing stage, it is especially important that you have an attorney.

10
TAXES

10 NOTE: This chapter primarily describes certain provisions of federal income tax laws in effect on January 1, 1990. Because of the complexity of the federal tax laws and the fact that such laws frequently change, you should not rely on this article in computing your federal tax liability or engaging in tax planning. This article is intended to provide very general information only. If you have any significant tax problems, you should consult your own tax advisor.

WHAT FACTORS PLAY A SIGNIFICANT ROLE IN DETERMINING MY TAX LIABILITY?

Your marital status plays a significant role in determining your tax liability. Relatedly, whether you have dependents for whom you can claim a personal exemption, explained later, and whether you maintain a household for a certain period of the year may also impact your tax liability. This chapter discusses some very basic provisions of federal income tax law that may affect you. Many of the tax provisions are relatively new, having been enacted as part of the Tax Reform Act of 1986 (1986 Act), which was a major overhaul of the nation's tax laws.

Where significant, the differences between the old law and the new law are discussed.

HOW DOES MY MARITAL STATUS AFFECT THE AMOUNT OF FEDERAL INCOME TAX I PAY?

Your filing status (or the tax class you fit into) is determined by your marital status. Your filing status is important because it controls the tax rates that are applied to your income and affects your eligibility for certain exemptions, deductions, and credits.

HOW DO I DETERMINE MY FILING STATUS?

You should determine whether you meet the criteria for one of the following filing classes on the last day of your tax year.[1]

Married Filing Joint Return: You may file under this classification if, on the last day of the tax year, any *one* of the following applies:

1. You are married and living as husband and wife;

2. You are living with a man in a common-law marriage recognized in the state where the marriage began;[2]

3. You are married and living apart, but you are not legally separated under a decree of divorce or separate maintenance; or

4. You are separated under an interlocutory decree of divorce.

You may file jointly whether or not both you and your husband had income and irrespective of the amount of such income.

Married Filing Separate Returns: If you and your husband are eligible to file joint returns, you may each file as a married person filing separate returns, whether or not both you and your husband had income. If you file separately, you should each report only your own income and claim only your own exemptions and deductions.

Surviving Spouse: If your husband dies, you may file a joint return for the year of his death. (This will give you lower tax rates than filing as a single person.) If you remarry before the end of the tax year in which your husband dies, you cannot file a joint return as the "surviving spouse" of your deceased husband, but you may file jointly with your new husband.

Head of Household: You may file as a head of household, and get the advantage of special rates, if you meet *all* of the following criteria:

1. You are unmarried;[3]

2. You maintain a household for more than half the tax year in which your children, grandchildren, stepchildren, or other persons who qualify you for a dependency deduction reside (if a child, grandchild, or stepchild is married, that child must be your dependent to qualify);

3. You pay over half the cost of maintaining the home; and

4. You are not a nonresident alien.

Single: If you are unmarried and do not qualify to file as a surviving spouse or head of household, you must file as a single taxpayer.

WHAT IS THE SIGNIFICANCE OF MY FILING STATUS?

Tax Rates: As discussed above and elsewhere in this article, your filing status affects the tax rate applied to your income in determining your tax liability.

Standard Deduction: Your filing status will determine the standard deduction for which you are eligible. The standard deduction, which is a flat allowance taken in place of itemized deductions, replaces the "zero bracket amount" that was repealed by the 1986 Act. (Itemized deductions are discussed later.) The zero bracket amount was built into the tax table and the tax rate schedule, which listed the tax above the zero bracket amount.

For 1990 the basic standard deduction is as follows:

Filing Status	1990 Amount
Single persons	$3,250
Heads of households	4,750
Married persons filing jointly	5,450
Surviving spouse	5,450
Married persons filing separately	2,725

Liability to File Return. Your filing status also affects whether or not you must file a return. In 1989, the gross income filing requirements were as follows:

Filing Status	1989 Gross Income
Married—joint return	$9,200
Married—separate return	2,000
Single (including divorced)	5,100
Surviving spouse	7,200
Head of household	6,550

Both the standard deduction and the gross income filing requirements are higher for people who are aged sixty-five or older or who are blind.

WHAT ARE THE ADVANTAGES AND DISADVANTAGES OF FILING A JOINT RETURN?

Filing a joint return generally yields a lower tax. This is because the tax rate is higher for married persons filing separately. Moreover, if you are married, unless you file a joint return, you cannot claim the child and dependent care credit, the earned income credit, or the tax credit for the elderly.

A disadvantage of filing a joint return is that you and your husband are not only jointly liable for the tax, but if your husband dies, disappears, or is incarcerated, each of you is separately liable for the entire tax.[5] The so-called "Innocent Spouse Provision"[6] in the Internal Revenue Code will relieve you from liability on a joint return in these limited circumstances:

1. There is a substantial understatement of tax which is attributable to "grossly erroneous items" (such as claims for deductions or credits made by your husband and for which there is no basis in fact or law); and

2. You can prove that you not only did not know about the understatement but had no reason to know of it; and

3. It would be inequitable to hold you liable for the tax deficiency in light of the circumstances.

Even though higher tax rates apply, filing a separate return is sometimes advantageous. If either you or your husband have substantial deductions that can only be claimed to the extent they exceed a certain percentage of adjusted gross income, filing separately may be advisable.[7] Medical expenses are deductible only to the extent they exceed 7.5 percent of adjusted gross income.[8] Casualty and theft loss deductions relating to nonbusiness property are deductible only to the extent they exceed 10 percent of adjusted gross income.[9] Moreover, numerous other miscellaneous itemized deductions, such as unreimbursed employee business expenses, expenses related to investment income and property, and tax return preparation costs are deductible only to the extent they exceed 2 percent of adjusted gross income.[10] If the spouse with these expenses has a low adjusted gross income and the other spouse has a high adjusted gross income, filing separate returns may be necessary in order to take the deduction for these expenses.

WHAT IS THE MARRIAGE PENALTY AND HOW DOES IT AFFECT ME?

The 1986 Act repealed the deduction for two-earner married couples. This deduction had been enacted in 1981 to offset the "marriage penalty." Marriage penalty is the term used to describe the tax
10
disadvantage that certain married couples have compared to single taxpayers. For example, in 1989, two single taxpayers could have a total of $37,100 in taxable income, all of which was subject to the 15 percent rate. If they were married, the 28 percent rate applied to amounts in excess of $30,950. Moreover, the 33 percent rate began at $74,850 on a joint return. Two unmarried taxpayers could have combined income of up to $93,130 before the 33 percent rate started to apply. Clearly the repeal of the deduction for two-earner married couples will adversely affect you if you have significant taxable income when combined with that of your husband.

HOW DOES MY MARITAL STATUS AFFECT THE NUMBER OF EXEMPTIONS I AM ALLOWED?

In computing your taxable income you may be eligible for one or more personal exemptions. Under the 1986 Act, the personal exemption amount for each individual was $1,950 in 1988 and $2,000 in 1989. In 1990 the $2,000 amount was adjusted for inflation. Starting in 1988, the benefit of the personal exemption was phased out for taxpayers whose taxable income exceeded specific levels. For example, married persons whose joint income in 1988 was $149,250 or greater lost part of their personal exemptions. There are personal exemptions for married persons and personal exemptions for dependents. These are discussed below.

Exemptions for Married Persons: If you are married, or separated but not under a final divorce decree or were widowed during the tax year and are not remarried, and you file a joint return, you and your husband may each claim an exemption of $2,000, or a total of $4,000.[11] If you, but not your husband, file a separate return, you may claim an exemption for your husband too if he had no income and was not someone else's dependent. If you and your husband file separately, then you may take only your exemption deduction on your return and he may take his exemption deduction on his return.[12]

If your husband dies during the tax year and you had no gross income, but were not the dependent of another, you may claim a $2,000 exemption for both you and your husband on the final return for your deceased spouse.[13]

Exemptions for Dependents: Five criteria must be met to claim the personal exemption for a dependent.

1. *Support*. Generally, you must furnish over 50 percent of a person's support to be entitled to a personal exemption for him or her. However, this requirement does not apply to a son, daughter, stepchild, adopted child, or foster child who is considered to be a ''student.''[14]

Special rules for determining support apply if you are legally divorced or separated or are separated under a written agreement. Generally, the parent who has custody for the greater period during the year is considered to have provided more than half of the child's support.[15] However, the noncustodial parent can claim the personal exemption if the custodial parent signs a written declaration that he or she will not claim the dependency exemption. A copy of the written agreement allocating the dependency exemption to the noncustodial parent must be attached to that parent's return.[16]

2. *Relationship*. The dependency exemption can be claimed for

most blood relatives, relatives by marriage, and legally adopted children. In addition, a person who used your household as a principal residence for the entire year may qualify as your dependent.[17]

3. *Gross Income Limit.* The dependent's gross income for the year must be less than the exemption amount, unless the dependent is your child *and* is either a student or has not reached age nineteen by the end of the year.[18]

4. *Joint Return.* You may not claim a dependency exemption for any taxpayer who files a joint return.[19]

5. *Citizenship or Residence.* The dependent must generally be a U.S. citizen or a resident of the U.S., Canada, or Mexico.[20]

WHAT DEDUCTIONS AND CREDITS MAY BE PARTICULARLY IMPORTANT TO ME AS A WOMAN TAXPAYER?

Certain deductions especially important to women include those for expenses related to divorce and for medical expenses.

During the course of a divorce, you may deduct fees charged by either a lawyer or an accountant for tax advice. However, you may not deduct legal fees for representation in the divorce, because these fees are considered to be personal expenses and most personal expenses are nondeductible. If you have to sue to get or collect alimony, you may be able to deduct the legal fees incurred in the suit as income-producing expenses.[21] (The deduction for tax advice and for costs of collecting alimony can be deducted only to the extent they exceed 2 percent of adjusted gross income.) You can deduct alimony or separate maintenance payments that you pay,[22] but no deductions are allowed for any property transferred as a result of the divorce. Moreover, no deduction is allowed for child support payments.

Expenses incurred in adopting a child, even a child with special needs, are no longer deductible.

Deductions are allowed for such medical expenses as contraceptives prescribed by your doctor,[23] legal abortions,[24] and voluntary sterilizations.[25] Care of a normal and healthy baby by a nurse, diaper services, etc., do not qualify as deductible medical expenses.[26] If your insurance paid for the medical service or you were otherwise reimbursed, you cannot take the deduction. As discussed above, medical expenses are deductible only to the extent they exceed 7.5 percent of your adjusted gross income. For further information, see "Deduction for Medical and Dental Expenses," Publication 502 of the Internal Revenue Service.

An important tax break for many working women is the dependent care credit.[27] If you are responsible for dependent care expenses, you may qualify for this credit. The expenses you incur must be paid for the care of a spouse or dependent who is incapable of self-care, or any person under age fifteen for whom you can claim a dependency exemption. (However, in the case of divorced parents, the custodial parent can claim the credit even if the noncustodial parent claims the child's dependency exemption.)

You can claim the credit only if you meet all of the following requirements:

1. You paid for the care so that you (and your husband if you were married) could work or look for work.

2. You and the qualifying person(s) lived in the same home.

3. You (and your husband if you were married) paid over half the cost of keeping up your home. The cost includes rent, mortgage interest, property taxes, utilities, home repairs, and food eaten at home.

4. The person you paid to provide the care was not your husband or a person you could claim as a dependent. If the person you paid to provide the care was your child, he or she must be at least nineteen years of age by the end of the tax year for which you are claiming the expense.

5. If you are considered "married" for federal income tax purposes, you must file a joint return with your husband to qualify for this credit. However, you can take the credit even if you do not file a joint return if

a. You were living apart from your husband during the last six months of the year, and

b. You provided over half the cost of maintaining a household that was the principal residence of the qualifying individual for over half of the year.

The amount of the child care credit is 30 percent of work-related expenses if your adjusted gross income is $10,000 or less. The 30 percent is reduced by 1 percent for each $2,000 of your adjusted gross income, or part of $2,000, above $10,000 until the percentage is reduced to 20 percent for income above $28,000. A chart for the applicable percentage is provided on Form 2441, "Credit for Child Care and Dependent Care Expenses." The maximum child care credit you can take to reduce your tax in any year is $720 if your expenses are for one qualifying individual or $1,440 if expenses are for two or more.

The credit is available to married couples if one works full-time and the other part-time or is a full-time student. The amount is limited to the earnings of the spouse with the lower income. If one spouse is a student or is incapable of self-care and so has no earned income, the law presumes an income of $200 per month if there is one dependent and $400 per month for two or more whether there is, in fact, any income at all. If, in the same month, both you and your husband were full-time students and did not work, you may not claim any income for that month on which to figure the credit. The same rule applies to a couple who did not work because neither was capable of

self-care.

WHAT KINDS OF INCOME MIGHT BE SIGNIFICANT TO ME AS A WOMAN TAXPAYER?

If you are receiving alimony or separate maintenance payments, you must pay tax on the payments.[28] Generally, there is no taxable gain or loss on the transfer of property as part of a divorce settlement. The transfer is treated as a tax-free gift.[29] (Transfers of property made as part of a divorce settlement which occurred prior to 19 July 1984 were generally taxable.[30]) See IRS Publication 504, "Tax Information for Divorced or Separated Individuals," for additional information.

Support for a minor child is not taxed as income to you; however, unless the divorce decree or separation agreement specifies an amount of child support, the entire payment you receive will be considered alimony.[31]

If you have an adopted child, payments you receive from a state agency to help you care for the child are not subject to income tax, but you can't count that money as child support you furnished in claiming a dependency exemption for that child.[32]

Awards in a Title VII suit are considered taxable "wages." (See chapter 2, "Employment.") Unemployment benefits from a private program are taxable to the extent the amounts you receive exceed the amounts you contributed to the program.[33] Amounts received as unemployment compensation under either a federal or state law are included in your taxable income.[34] (Before 1987, a limited amount of unemployment compensation was excludable from gross income.)

A limited part of Social Security benefits is taxable if an individual's adjusted gross income plus one-half of the Social Security benefits received during the year exceeds certain "base amounts." The base amounts are $32,000 for married persons filing jointly; $0 for married persons filing separately who do not live apart at all times during the year; and $25,000 for all other individuals.[35] No more than half the benefits are taxed. To avoid having a penalty imposed for failure to pay estimated tax, individuals whose benefits are taxable may need to file and pay quarterly estimated taxes on Form 1040-ES, Estimated Tax for Individuals.

For more information on the new tax on some Social Security benefits and on estimated taxes, see Publication 505, "Tax Withholding and Estimated Tax."

Babysitting income, tips, and gratuities are also taxable income. If you are a widow, proceeds of a life insurance policy on your husband's life are not taxable income.[36] Certain death benefits that your deceased husband's employer may pay you are taxed only to the extent that the payment exceeds $5,000.[37] If you are the executor of your husband's estate, your fees, if any, are taxable income.

If you or your husband serve in the military, Family Separation Allowances received because of overseas assignments are excluded from your taxable income.[38] If you are the widow of a serviceman who died in active service, death gratuity benefits you receive from the government are not taxable,[39] nor are benefits you receive under any law administered by the Veterans' Administration.[40]

WHERE CAN I GET MORE INFORMATION ON FEDERAL INCOME TAXES?

Federal income tax forms contain detailed instructions. The IRS also publishes a series of free pamphlets, the Taxpayer Information Series, available at your local IRS office. Call your local IRS office or call the toll-free number listed in your telephone directory.

WHAT ABOUT UTAH INCOME TAX LAWS?

Utah income tax liability is computed in substantially the same manner as federal income tax liability. The Utah state income tax return takes most figures for computing Utah income tax directly off your federal income tax return, but some adjustments are required in certain figures taken off the federal return. The number of personal exemptions allowable is the same as those permitted under federal tax law. The amount excluded from income per exemption is 75 percent of the federal personal exemption. For 1989, this was $1,500 per person.

In Utah, married taxpayers may file jointly or separately; but if you filed separate federal income tax returns, you must file separate returns in Utah. If you filed a joint federal return, you can choose to file separate Utah returns, dividing up nonbusiness deductions as you like. This includes a division of personal exemptions for a dependent child or relative.

WHAT UTAH PROPERTY TAXES MUST I PAY?

Real property and certain limited classes of personal property in Utah are taxed by the county in which you live. For example, you pay the county assessor taxes on your car (personal) and your house (real) every year.

WHEN MUST I PAY TAXES ON GIFTS?

You are not liable for any tax as a result of receiving a gift. However, if you give a gift during your lifetime, or arrange for the transfer of property to your heirs following your death, federal estate and gift taxes may be owing. You are allowed a unified credit of $192,800 against federal gift and estate taxes. This means you can transfer $600,000 worth of property during your lifetime and at death before you or your estate will incur any tax liability.[41]

11

MONEY PROBLEMS AND BANKRUPTCY

WHAT IS BANKRUPTCY?

In common speech, we say someone is bankrupt when she is overburdened by her financial obligations and cannot pay all of her bills. Bankruptcy as a legal state is a court's declaration that you cannot pay and cannot be held accountable to your creditors except through the court.

Congress enacted the Federal Bankruptcy Code[1] to help individuals, partnerships, or corporations who can no longer meet their financial obligations.

HOW DOES BANKRUPTCY AFFECT ME?

Bankruptcy laws can affect you in various ways. You might find yourself in a position where you cannot pay your bills or make loan or mortgage payments, or you might receive notice from the court that a person, partnership, or corporation who owes *you* money has filed for relief under the Bankruptcy Code.

Before taking any action on the information contained in this chapter, you should consult an attorney who is experienced in bankruptcy law. A lawyer can give you more specific and individualized assistance about your alternatives whether you owe money or someone owes you money. Even if you feel you cannot afford an attorney's services, you should at least seek a consultation with one to explain the law to you.

The Utah State Bar's Lawyer Referral Office (531-9075) will refer you to a lawyer who will meet with you for $15 for the first thirty-minute visit. The Utah State Bar also can arrange an initial consultation through its Tuesday Night Bar Committee.

AM I A CREDITOR?

You are a "creditor"[2] of a "debtor"[3] (someone in debt to you) under the Bankruptcy Code when you have a "claim,"[4] or a right to payment from someone who has declared bankruptcy.

Often the first time you learn that someone who owes you money has filed bankruptcy is when you receive in the mail a document called "Order for Relief and Notice of First Meeting of Creditors." The person who owes you money is required to list the names and addresses of all his or her creditors so that they can be given written notice. When bankruptcy papers are filed, an "automatic stay"[5] goes into effect which stops, among other things, all efforts to collect money owed.

You can go to the first meeting of creditors, ask the debtor questions, and hear what the debtor, his or her attorney, and the trustee have to say about how the case will proceed. The trustee is chosen by the Bankruptcy Court from a panel of trustees and is an officer of the court, not an attorney for either side. His or her name is always given on the "Order for Relief."

If you are a creditor of someone you discover has filed bankruptcy and you have not received any notice in the mail, you should immediately go to the clerk of the Bankruptcy Court. In Salt Lake City it is in Room 361, U.S. Courthouse at 350 South Main Street. Look at the debtor's file to see if (or how) you are listed as a creditor, and contact an attorney for advice about your legal rights and remedies.

WHAT CAN I DO TO GET MY MONEY FROM SOMEONE WHO DECLARES BANKRUPTCY?

If someone owes you money, you will want to do everything you can legally do to protect and collect your claim. This is the reason you should consult an attorney who is knowledgeable in bankruptcy law.

The person who owes money can request relief under the Bankruptcy Code in several different ways. (See below, ''What Types of Procedures Does the Bankruptcy Code Provide?'') Generally, your rights and remedies under the code depend on the type of proceedings the debtor chooses.

In most cases, in order to protect your claim, you or your attorney should quickly file a Proof of Claim in the debtor's case. In the Proof of Claim, you explain the reason the debtor owes you money, what that amount is, and identify any lien[6] or security[7] for your claim.

A lien or security is usually ''real property,'' such as land and buildings, or ''personal property,'' such as cars, jewelry, or furniture. Another word for *lien* or *security* is *collateral*. If you have a lien or security for your claim, you may, in some situations, get authorization from the Bankruptcy Court to get your property back from the debtor in exchange for giving up part or all of your claim. Again, it is important that you hire an attorney to do this for you as the required proceedings are very technical and often complex.

If you are the landlord of a debtor, you have a right to collect ongoing rents from the debtor which become due after the date his bankruptcy was filed. Again, since the procedures for accomplishing this are technical, you should consult an attorney immediately.

To best protect your claim against the debtor, *do not delay*. You should promptly consult an attorney, file a Proof of Claim, and keep informed of the progress of the case. Most bankruptcy cases are resolved quickly, within three to six months after the first filing. Others, depending on their complexity, can take much longer. In almost every case, interested creditors can help move the case along.

WILL I GET MY MONEY BACK FROM A DEBTOR WHO DECLARES BANKRUPTCY?

Whether you will get your money back from a debtor who declares bankruptcy depends on what kind of claim you have. For example, if the bankruptcy is a Chapter 7 (these types are explained later in this chapter), unsecured creditors get paid nothing if the court determines that there are no assets from which creditors may be paid. If it is a Chapter 11 or a Chapter 13 bankruptcy and the person owes you wages, you will be paid first. If you have a secured claim, you will either be paid the presently determined fair value for the item through the plan or you will get the security back. For instance, if you sold a car to X who subsequently declared bankruptcy and still owes you $1,500 on the car worth $1,000, you'll either get paid $1,000 through the plan or you'll get the car back. If the debtor keeps the car and pays $1,000, your claim for $500 goes into a pot with all the other claims and you will be paid proportionally with all the other creditors (pro rata).

WHAT SHOULD I KNOW IF I BECOME A DEBTOR?

If you find that you cannot pay your bills and your creditors are pressuring you, you may wish to consider one of the kinds of debt relief provided by the Bankruptcy Code to give yourself a chance for a fresh start.

11 You should know that there are some alternatives to declaring bankruptcy. You can sometimes work out an arrangement with individual creditors to pay in certain installments. However, if you have signed a note agreeing to pay $150 on some furniture by the 15th of each month, it may not matter that you work out an arrangement to pay $75 for twice as long. If the creditor chooses, he or she can legally sue on the basis of the written document. The alternative arrangement will not be legally binding unless you also put it into writing.

If a creditor refuses to negotiate with you or to make some arrangement for payment, you can consult a credit counseling service listed in the yellow pages. Their services are sometimes helpful in explaining different options to you and in helping you to work out arrangements with creditors. Under the state law, you and your creditors can voluntarily agree to a repayment plan with the same terms as a court-ordered "reorganization" (Chapter 11) or Chapter 13 plan. However, if even one creditor refuses to go along with this arrangement, it is not binding on any of them.

It is unwise to try to work out this kind of arrangement without a lawyer, since the statute is very complicated.

Even though the great advantage of bankruptcy is that it lets you start over again with a clean slate, there are some disadvantages that make other repayment arrangements worth considering. Your reputation suffers and the declaration of bankruptcy will be reported on your credit history. It is not a cheap or easy way to get yourself out of a minor financial hole.

WHAT TYPES OF PROCEDURES DOES THE BANKRUPTCY CODE PROVIDE?

Bankruptcy proceedings may be either voluntary or involuntary. "Voluntary" means that you have taken the initiative yourself to seek this form of relief. In contrast, your creditors may begin an "involuntary" proceeding. This usually happens only when debts are connected to a business. Few creditors launch bankruptcy proceedings to collect personal accounts.

You can be subjected to a great deal of pressure, however, when you owe someone money. If someone has lent you money on your car or your furniture, they can take those things away from you. They can take you to court directly or refer the case to a collection agency who will sue you in a state court for a percentage of the money owed. If the sum is small enough, they can take you to a small claims court. If you ran up the debt on a credit card, your bank or the store can cancel your credit with them.

There are, however, some restrictions on what a creditor or collection agency can do. They are not allowed to call you at the office if you ask them not to and they cannot call during normal sleeping hours. Neither can they exaggerate the legal consequences of what will happen to you if you do not pay.

Chapter 7

The Bankruptcy Code offers various types of proceedings. One is a Chapter 7 liquidation proceeding ("Chapter" refers to part of the code). This process authorizes the trustee to gather together all your nonexempt assets and sell them, or "liquidate" them for cash. ("Exempt" assets are those which cannot be reached by your creditors.[8]) In Utah, the exemptions you may claim in bankruptcy are provided for by state law.[9]

When you talk to an attorney, he or she will tell you about the list of exempt items. This list includes some furniture, basic household appliances like a refrigerator, washer and dryer, clothing, and sometimes some heirlooms. The statute also specifies the dollar amounts of the exemptions. If you use a car in your business or profession, it is exempt up to $1,500. (Driving back and forth to work is considered personal use, not professional use; a plumber's truck would be considered a professional-use vehicle.) The tools of your trade are exempt up to $1,500. You can keep $500 worth of furniture, $500 worth of animals, books, and musical instruments, and $500 worth of heirlooms or sentimental items.

The statute also specifies a "right of homestead," or the right of a person to live in a house and have a value retained in that house. A head of household can have a value of $8,000 in a house, a spouse can have $2,000, and $500 can be claimed for each dependent. If you have a mortgage on the house, the homestead right does not apply except on the equity. If your house is worth $50,000 and you have a first mortgage of $20,000, you deduct the homestead allowance from the $30,000 difference or equity. Alimony, support, and maintenance are also exempt from claims of creditors. See the State Exemption Statute for a complete list.

If the trustee decides to liquidate your nonexempt assets, the cash thus raised will be distributed among your unsecured creditors (those who do not have a lien or security) on a pro-rata basis. That is, each creditor will receive an amount of cash proportionate to the size of that creditor's claim against you. If your only assets are exempt or of nominal value, the trustee will probably close your case as a "no-asset" case, and your creditors will receive nothing on their claims. A Chapter 7 liquidation proceeding may be either voluntary or involuntary.

Chapter 13

Another alternative provided by the code is known as a Chapter 13 or "Adjustment of Debts of an Individual with Regular Income."

Basically, this method allows someone with regular income (such as wages or any form of government payments or assistance) to work out a plan to pay off her outstanding debts, in full or in part, over a specified period of time no longer than sixty months. A bankruptcy judge must "confirm" the plan before it goes into effect.

Chapter 13 can solve the problem of curing delinquencies in your mortgage and the orderly payment of secured debts along with your unsecured debts. Most mortgages and secured debts provide for foreclosure and repossession if you fall behind on your monthly payments. Chapter 13 allows you to make the current payments and make up the delinquencies (cure the default) over the time of the plan without risking foreclosure or repossession.

Once the plan has been confirmed by the bankruptcy judge, the creditors have no choice. They have to accept it and so do you. If you fail to pay on schedule, the trustee files a motion. The motion will ask that the matter be converted to a Chapter 7 (see the above section), or that it be dismissed. If it is dismissed, then it is a race to the courthouse for the creditors, since the first one with a judgment against you can get your nonexempt property.

Note that you are the only one who can file a Chapter 13; your creditors cannot force you to accept such a plan. You also have a right to "convert" this proceeding into a Chapter 7 liquidation bankruptcy at any point, but your creditors cannot convert it unless you default.

Chapter 11

The code also provides for a Chapter 11, "Reorganization of Debt," proceeding. This chapter is most commonly used by businesses (corporations or partnerships) and allows the business to remain in operation. The debtor proposes a payment plan for her creditors, which must be confirmed by the bankruptcy judge after creditors have had a chance to vote for or against it.

WHAT IS THE PROCEDURE FOR VOLUNTARY FILING?

You must file a petition with the Bankruptcy Court and pay a $90 fee for either a Chapter 7 or a Chapter 13. The fee for a Chapter 11 is $500. Payment of this fee is mandatory, but under some circumstances it may be paid in installments.

You and your husband may decide to file a joint case[10] if you are both responsible for your debts and own most of your property together. This procedure is designed to reduce legal and court costs and allow a speedier decision. Under this procedure you are required to pay only one filing fee.

After your petition has been filed, the court will issue an ''Order for Relief'' and the ''automatic stay'' described above goes into effect. This means that all collection efforts, harassment, and lawsuits against you cease immediately. This gives you a breathing spell from your creditors' attempts to collect from you. In a Chapter 13 proceeding, the ''automatic stay'' provision also protects your codebtors who have not filed petitions in bankruptcy.[11] For example, for nonbusiness debts like personal items, family expenses, or household expenses where someone cosigns with you, until the creditor files a request with the court for permission to collect from the cosigner, your Chapter 13 protects the cosigner against the creditor, too. Cosigning on a business loan would not be protected.

WHAT HAPPENS TO ME, MY ASSETS, AND MY DEBTS IF I CHOOSE A CHAPTER 7?

If you choose a Chapter 7 liquidation bankruptcy, a trustee is appointed by the court to ''collect'' your assets under the supervision of a bankruptcy judge. The trustee has the right to inventory and evaluate all of your property to see if it may be used to pay your debts. But you are permitted to claim certain property as ''exempt,'' or beyond the reach of your creditors.

Once your nonexempt assets (if any) have been collected, or ''liquidated,'' and the cash from the sale distributed among your creditors (or if the trustee decides yours is a ''no-asset'' case), you will usually be granted a ''discharge''[12] of your outstanding debts. Once you have been discharged you have no legal obligation to pay these debts. There are, however, a few important exceptions.[13] A person who declares bankruptcy must still pay alimony or child support if he or she had that obligation. You must still pay some other types of obligations, like student loans or debts you acquire through false pretenses or the use of a false written statement,[14] or certain taxes.[15]

The ''discharge'' is designed to give you a fresh start. In effect, the slate is wiped clean of your past debts.[16] To encourage the fresh start, the code says that no government office can discriminate against you just because you have gone through a bankruptcy proceeding. This means you cannot lose your job, whether with the government or private industry, or be denied a driver's license or other license solely because of your bankruptcy.[17]

WHAT'S A REAFFIRMATION?

Even though you have "discharge" and an opportunity for a new beginning, you may decide to "reaffirm" your legal obligation to pay a particular debt.[18] You make this decision for a variety of reasons. If the "reaffirmation" involves a consumer debt, like a TV from a department store, the reaffirmation agreement must be in writing, signed by the creditor, you, and your attorney, and it must be filed with the court before your discharge is granted. Only after you take all these steps will you be legally required to pay that particular debt as though the discharge had never occurred. Of course, you may decide voluntarily to pay some or all of the debts from which you are discharged, but you are not legally obligated to do so, nor can your creditors require you to do so.

Reaffirming is completely voluntary on the debtor's part. If you are a creditor and there is a possibility of reaffirmation, it is important that you get legal advice immediately.

WHAT IF I DECIDE TO TRY A CHAPTER 13?

As discussed earlier, the Chapter 7 liquidation is just one of your alternatives. You may decide to use the Chapter 13 proceeding instead. If you choose this alternative you will be allowed to keep your property and pay your debts through the plan you work out with the trustee and your creditors. In many cases, the bankruptcy court will simply order your employer to make a payroll deduction from your wages in the amount required in the "confirmed" Chapter 13 plan. That amount goes directly to the Chapter 13 trustee who will send payments to your creditors according to your individual plan.

After all payments provided by your Chapter 13 plan have been made (over a period of time no longer than sixty months), you will receive a "discharge" from all debts included in the plan.[19] This gives you a clean slate except for obligations for taxes, alimony, child support, and mortgage or other long-term secured obligations. Under a

Chapter 11 or 7 bankruptcy, you cannot be discharged from all debts. You are still responsible for debt incurred through false pretenses, embezzlement, torts (a fine you have been ordered to pay for beating someone up, for instance), and student loans. If you are not able to perform according to your Chapter 13 plan because of "hardship" (for example, you lose your job or get sick), the court could grant you the same discharge you would receive under Chapter 7.

WHAT EFFECT WILL BANKRUPTCY HAVE ON MY ABILITY TO OBTAIN CREDIT?

Ironically, you may be viewed by some creditors as a good credit risk once you have gone through the proceeding. This is because the code says that unless you have paid back at least 70 percent of your unsecured debts in a Chapter 13 case, you may not be granted another "discharge" of debts for at least six years.[20] Other creditors, however, may be reluctant to give you credit and may, in fact, lawfully refuse you credit because of your previous record. The fact of your bankruptcy may remain a part of your credit history for as long as fourteen years under the terms of the Fair Credit Reporting Act. As a result, you may experience difficulty in getting credit except where high rates of interest are charged. This is a significant result of bankruptcy and one you should think about carefully before you decide to file a petition.

11

CAN A CREDITOR DENY ME CREDIT BECAUSE OF MY HUSBAND'S BANKRUPTCY?

If you did not file a joint bankruptcy petition with your husband and you are applying for an unsecured loan which you alone are responsible for repaying, a creditor may not legally deny you the loan because of your husband's bankruptcy.

HOW MUCH WILL IT COST ME TO FILE BANKRUPTCY?

First there are the filing fees: $90 for a joint petition under Chapters 7 and 13. A Chapter 11 reorganization fee is $500. Legal fees are in addition to that. Attorneys generally charge for services based upon hourly rates, and the total fee depends on the complexity of the case. In Chapter 7 cases, you usually have to pay the fees immediately. If you file a Chapter 13 bankruptcy, you can sometimes pay part of it and negotiate an arrangement to have the rest paid in installments out of your monthly payments along with the other creditors. In all cases, the fees have to be approved by the court. You must usually give your attorney a retainer when you employ his or her services. This retainer will be disclosed to the court; final fees are submitted to and approved by the court before payment.

12

JURY DUTY AND VOTING RIGHTS

HOW ARE JURORS SELECTED?

Under Utah law, prospective jurors for county and state courts are selected county by county from the official register of voters for each voting district in the county and from persons in the jurisdiction who have a Utah driver's license. This master list is periodically updated to include the names of persons registered to vote in the most recent general election and new holders of drivers' licenses. Thus, if you are registered to vote or lawfully drive a vehicle, your name is on the master list and you are eligible to be called as a juror. The master list may be supplemented by names from other sources as directed by the Utah Supreme Court, which has required only since January 1, 1988, that licensed drivers become part of the master list.

Prospective jurors are to be selected at random from a fair cross-section of the population of the area served by the court. No citizen may be excluded or exempted from jury duty because of race, color, religion, sex, national origin, or economic status.

AM I QUALIFIED TO BE A JUROR?

Not everyone on the master list is qualified to serve as a juror. Utah law requires that jurors be citizens of the United States, over eighteen years of age, registered to vote, residents of the county, and able to read, speak, and understand English. The court determines whether prospective jurors are qualified. It bases its decision on the information provided on the juror qualification forms, interviews with prospective jurors, and other evidence as needed. Furthermore, a person may *not* serve who has been convicted of a felony, is on active duty in the military, or is incapable of rendering satisfactory jury service because of physical or mental disability.

IF I AM SELECTED, WHAT IS THE PROCEDURE?

You will receive in the mail a juror qualification form from the clerk of the court. The purpose of this form is to let the court determine whether you are qualified to serve as a juror based on the seven requirements shown above. You must complete and return this form to the clerk within ten days after it is received, *even if you think you are not qualified to serve as a juror*. The court will make this determination. If you have a mental or physical disability, you may be required to submit a physician's certificate to verify it.

Any person who fails to complete and return a jury qualification form or who willfully misrepresents a material fact on the form may be fined up to $500 and/or imprisoned for up to thirty days.

MAY I BE EXCUSED FROM JURY DUTY?

Jury duty is one of a citizen's responsibilities—and a very important one. As a juror, you represent the community in determining guilt or innocence in the cases you will hear. However, under certain circumstances, you may be excused from jury duty even if you are otherwise qualified.

To be excused, you must show undue hardship, extreme inconvenience, or public necessity. For example, an excuse of severe illness in your immediate family that requires your presence at home will usually be sustained. Or if you own your own business and receive a call to jury duty during your busiest season, you can usually be excused or at least have your time of jury service postponed. Should your job be one of public necessity (important to the day-to-day functioning of the community) like that of a doctor or fireman, you can request to be excused from jury service. It is up to the court to decide, based on your request, whether or not to excuse you.

WHAT ABOUT JURY DUTY IN FEDERAL COURTS?

Any qualified citizen can be called to serve on a jury for a federal as well as a state or county court. The selection process is basically the same. From the list of voters who voted in the last general election, the county jury commission composes a master list of prospective jurors. At the request of a judge, the clerk of the court randomly selects a panel of jurors from the master list and sends each of them a juror qualification form to fill out.

However, in addition to the qualifications of the state courts, a juror in a federal court must have lived in the judicial district for at least a year. Also, anyone with a charge pending against her or him in a state or federal court of record for a crime punishable by imprisonment for more than a year is not qualified. You are exempt from federal court jury duty if you are in active service in the armed forces, in a police or fire department, or are a public official—elected or appointed, actively performing official duties in executive, legislative, or judicial offices of federal, state, or local governments. For instance, if you are a county recorder, you are exempt. If you are a secretary in the county recorder's office, however, you are eligible.

12 You may also be excused by individual request showing that jury service would create ''extreme inconvenience or undue hardship'' for you. For example, if you have to spend more than an hour traveling to court you would probably be excused. A mother of young children can usually be excused. For other examples of extreme inconvenience and undue hardship, please refer to the preceding section of this chapter entitled ''May I Be Excused from Jury Duty?''

ARE THERE OTHER REASONS I MAY NOT BE SELECTED?

You may be qualified and offer no excuses but still be excluded from serving on the jury of a particular case. You and the other prospective jurors are placed under oath and questioned by the judge and/or lawyers to determine your qualifications to serve as jurors for the case about to be tried. The purpose of this *voir dire* examination is to obtain an impartial, unbiased jury. Following *voir dire,* the final selection of the jury begins. The lawyers for each side "challenge" the jurors they find objectionable to their side.

A challenge is a request that a juror be excused. Challenges are either "for cause" or "peremptory." A challenge for cause is based upon some specific fact known about a juror which disqualifies him or her for the case at hand. Some possible reasons for which you might be challenged for cause include your having had a prior relationship with one of the parties, your prejudice or prior knowledge regarding the case, or the fact that you may stand to benefit in some way by a decision for one side or the other. There is no limit to the number of challenges for cause, but the judge decides whether to accept or reject each one.

A peremptory challenge can be made for no reason at all. Lawyers rely on their experience and "hunches" as to the type of juror who would be best for each client's case. A lawyer may excuse you peremptorily simply because he dislikes the way you sit or smile. Unlike challenges for cause, the number of peremptory challenges is strictly limited by law.

WHAT KINDS OF CASES COULD I BE ASKED TO SERVE ON?

Juries in Utah hear both criminal and civil cases. Criminal cases are controversies between the state and an accused individual. Civil cases are controversies between individuals concerning matters like contracts, accidents, debts, etc. In criminal cases, juries decide whether the accused is guilty and in capital cases only decide the punishment: life or death. Upon a guilty verdict, the judge, in most cases, determines what the sentence will be. In civil cases, juries decide not only who the winner is, but how much he or she wins.

A jury trial may last a few hours, a day, a week, several weeks, or, on rare occasions, several months. Jurors are not ordinarily sequestered (isolated from contact with the public) in Utah. They are allowed to go home at night during the trial but are cautioned not to read newspapers, watch television, or discuss the trial with anyone.

The same jury panel never hears more than one case, although individual jurors may serve on more than one jury during their term of jury service.

WHAT IF I GET SICK WHILE I'M SERVING?

You would, of course, be excused from jury duty should you become ill during the trial. What happens next depends on the type of case your jury is deciding.

In a lengthy felony case, Utah law provides for an alternate juror. The alternate is selected at the same time and in the same manner as the original jurors. He or she must attend the trial at all times and see and hear everything the original jurors do. If an original juror dies or becomes ill before the case is submitted to the jury for a decision, the alternate juror assumes the juror's place and is bound by the same rules.

Utah law requires unanimous jury verdicts in criminal cases. So, in a criminal trial where no alternate juror has been selected, the illness of a juror could result in a mistrial. This means that the lawyers would have to appear again at a later date, select a new jury, and present their case all over again.

In civil cases, only three-fourths of the jurors are required to reach a verdict, so the illness of one juror does not necessarily result in a mistrial.

HOW WILL JURY SERVICE AFFECT MY JOB?

Although some employers may choose not to pay a worker his or her wages while he or she serves as a juror, Utah law forbids your employer from threatening, coercing, or firing you because you are either called as a juror or serve on a jury. If your employer threatens to fire you or fires you when you are summoned for jury duty, you should contact a lawyer. Your employer could be held in criminal contempt, which could result in a fine of up to $500 and/or up to six months in prison. If your employer fires you, you may bring a civil suit within thirty days to obtain your wages and an order reinstating you in your job.

WILL I BE COMPENSATED FOR JURY DUTY?

Yes, you will receive fifteen cents a mile for travel from home to court and back. You will also receive $14 a day for each day you are required to attend court sessions.

HOW OFTEN AM I ELIGIBLE FOR JURY DUTY?

If you are being considered as a prospective juror, you are required to attend only ten court days (usually Mondays through Fridays, excluding holidays). If you are selected for a jury, however, you must complete your service for that particular case.

If you serve on a trial jury or a grand jury (which is a jury called to decide whether there is enough evidence to require an accused person to stand trial), you are not eligible to serve again for two years.

HOW DO I REGISTER AND VOTE?

To vote in an election, you must register to vote in the precinct in which you currently live at least thirty days before the election. If you are not registered to vote, contact your county registrar's office, which is listed under Voter Registration or Registration and Election Commission for your county. Sometimes voter registration is conducted in public places such as shopping centers. Under certain circumstances, you can even register by mail.

You no longer have to present your voter's registration card to vote in your precinct. As long as you are registered, you can vote upon showing a valid driver's license or Highway Department photo I.D.

13
WOMEN AND THE MILITARY

WHAT DOES THE MILITARY HAVE TO DO WITH ME?

Women may interact with the military in a number of ways. You may become involved as an active duty member of one of the armed services, join the reserves or national guard, or be the wife or dependent of an active duty member. In each instance, you will have certain rights and benefits. This chapter highlights some pertinent areas.

Remember that military recruiters will give you additional information, but their job is to get you to join. Therefore, they may paint an overly rosy picture. The VA office nearest your home can also provide information on benefits for former members of the military.

CAN I BE DRAFTED?

The draft was abolished in this country in 1973. This means that under *existing* legislation, neither women nor men can be drafted into military service.

In 1981, Congress approved legislation requiring all male United

States citizens and resident aliens in a certain age group to register under the Military Selective Service Act unless they were exempt for medical or other reasons. Although no laws prohibit registering women for military service, Congress has never chosen to do so. The United States Supreme Court has ruled that exempting women from registration for the draft is not unconstitutional. That is, it *is* legal to draft men and not to draft women.

These registration laws are presumably intended to give the military a list of eligible candidates who may be called for active service should Congress reinstate the draft. Congress would have to pass new legislation to require women to register with the selective service. Additional legislation would also be needed to reestablish the draft for men or women.

WHAT POSITIONS MAY I HOLD IN THE MILITARY?

Even though the military has traditionally been an exclusively male organization, recent years have seen dramatic changes. Today, women constitute 10 percent of the active force and 1.7 percent of the reserve components. As officers and enlisted personnel filling traditional and nontraditional roles, they serve in a wide variety of jobs. Equal opportunity for women, as well as minorities, is an integral part of policy for the military today. The Army's policy illustrates that of the other services:

> A. The policy of the United States Army is to provide equal opportunity and treatment for uniformed members and their families irrespective of race, color, religion, sex, or national origin and to provide an environment free of sexual harassment. This policy—
>
> 1. Applies both on and off post.
>
> 2. Extends to soldiers and their families.
>
> 3. Applies to soldiers' working, living, and recreation environments (including both on- and off-post housing).
>
> B. Soldiers will not be accessed, classified, trained, assigned, promoted, or be otherwise managed on the basis of race, color, religion, sex, or national origin except:

> 1. As the direct combat probability coding policy applies to women. . . . (U.S. Army Regulations 600–20 dated 1978, revised 15 Oct. 1980.)[1]

This exception currently prohibits women from serving in combat-related military occupational specialties (MOS). A few MOS's closed to women include infantryman, combat engineer, and atomic demolition munitions specialist.

The prohibition has extended to assigning women to combat units as well. In the naval service, women may be assigned to noncombatant ships which provide various support elements to United States Navy warships. Currently, women may not be assigned to warships. Women may attend the Navy, Army, and Air Force academies. They may also become military officers through ROTC programs or Officer Candidate School (OCS). With the equal opportunity policies of today's military, career paths have never been better for women in the armed services, whether it be as an officer or enlisted person.

WHAT ABOUT SEXUAL HARASSMENT?

Because of the traditional male military environment, women in the armed services have suffered instances of sexual harassment. In this regard, the military is a mirror of the rest of society. The military has taken an active role in fighting sexual harassment. Army policy is typical of that in all the services:

> Sexual harassment is an unwelcome form of sex discrimination. It is not limited to the work environment and can occur almost anywhere. Sexual harassment violates acceptable standards of integrity and impartiality required of all Army personnel and interferes with mission accomplishment and unit cohesion. Many of the acts and neglects that constitute sexual harassment are prohibited and are punishable under civil and military law as criminal acts of a sexual nature, and should be treated as such. Any military member or civilian employee is engaging in sexual harassment who—
>
> A. Through behavior of a sexual nature attempts to control, influence, or affect the career, pay, or job of a military member or civilian employee.

B. Makes deliberate or repeated verbal comments or gestures of a sexual nature that are offensive to the person to whom addressed.

C. Makes abusive physical contact of a sexual nature. (U.S. Army Regulation 600-21 dated 1 Feb. 1984.)

Women in the military are encouraged to report acts of sexual harassment. Military authorities are instructed to take immediate action to investigate and eliminate such demoralizing behavior.

WHAT IS FRATERNIZATION?

Closely allied to the problem of sexual harassment is fraternization. Although fraternization has not always been clearly defined, it basically involves improper relationships between senior and junior ranking individuals.

The Navy has recently issued a policy which explains its views on the subject.

Definitions

A. *Fraternization* is (1) any personal relationship between an officer and an enlisted member which is unduly familiar and does not respect differences in rank and grade; (2) any personal relationship between officers or between enlisted personnel which is unduly familiar and does not respect differences in rank and grade where a senior-subordinate supervisory relationship exists.

B. *''Senior-subordinate''* refers to the military relationship between members, including members of different services, in which one is senior to the other by virtue of grade, rank, or authority.

Prohibited relationships

A. *General:* (1) Fraternization, as defined above, is punishable as an offense under the Uniform Code of Military Justice when it is prejudicial to good order and discipline or brings discredit to the naval service. It is impossible to set forth every act that may be prejudicial to good order and discipline or is service-discrediting, because the surrounding circumstances often have more to do with making the act criminal than the act itself. However, dating, cohabitation, or sexual intimacy between an officer and an enlisted member is clearly inappropriate, as would be a private business partnership between an officer and an enlisted member. Likewise, such conduct between an officer and between enlisted personnel where a senior-subordinate supervisory relationship exists is equally inappropriate. (2) Conduct which constitutes fraternization is not excused by a subsequent marriage between the offending parties.

B. *Marriage and family relationships*: Service members who are married or otherwise related (a father and daughter, etc.) to other service members must maintain the requisite respect and decorum attending the official relationship while either is on duty or in uniform in public.

C. *Assignment policy*: Compatible with sea/shore rotation policy and the needs of the service, service members married to each other will not be assigned to the same chain of command.

Fraternization is a gender-neutral concept, focusing on the senior-subordinate relationship. It is, in this sense, a uniquely military concept.

IS IT MORE DIFFICULT TO GET MARRIED IF I AM IN THE MILITARY?

It is important to understand that military policy and national security take precedence over the needs of individuals. If you join the service and subsequently marry a serviceman, there is no guarantee that you will continue to be assigned to the same duty stations. Some of the services try to transfer couples together, but they are not required to do so. The key word is need: where do they need you?

If you become pregnant on active duty, you may seek a voluntary honorable discharge and it will be granted, regardless of your marital status. However, you cannot be involuntarily discharged from the service merely because you are pregnant, married or not. You must remember that when you join the service, you sign a legally binding contract that obligates you for a specific number of years. After you join, it is very difficult to get out until you have successfully completed your tour of duty. Early discharges often result in an unfavorable military discharge and/or record which can follow you for life. Hence, you should make a decision to join the military and/or marry in the military only after careful deliberation.

WHAT EFFECT MIGHT A DIVORCE HAVE ON MILITARY RETIRED PAY?

For many years, wives of servicemen could not claim any property interest in the retirement benefits their husbands earned. This was perceived as a gross inequity. In 1982 Congress enacted the Uniformed Services Former Spouses Protection Act,[2] effective 1 February 1983, which allows state courts to consider retired pay of military personnel when adjudicating property rights between parties in a divorce proceeding. Here are its key provisions:

The act does not require you to have been married for a minimum period before a state court is entitled to divide military retired pay.

The act provides that up to 50 percent of retired pay may be awarded as either marital or community property in a single divorce case.

Once you receive a court-ordered interest in retired pay, it becomes a lifetime interest. Even if you remarry, you will still receive it. In some cases for marriages of over ten years, the act lets the military send the check directly to you.

You are entitled to full medical, commissary, and exchange rights if your marriage lasted through twenty years of military service. However, courts cannot order that you be designated beneficiary under the Survivor Benefit Plan (SBP).

The act may be applied retroactively. Divorce judgments within a division of retired pay rendered before 26 June 1981 may now be enforced. Divorce judgments decided after that date without a division of retired pay may now be modified to include it.

IS DIVORCE LEGALLY DIFFERENT IN THE MILITARY?

No. Support orders, alimony, and child support can be and are enforced against military pay.

WHAT IS THE SOLDIERS' AND SAILORS' CIVIL RELIEF ACT?

Congress enacted this act at the beginning of World War II to help civilians mobilized into the military, either voluntarily or involuntarily.[3] The basic idea is not to penalize you because you are in military service; at the same time, you should not have an unfair advantage because of it.

Some of its benefits apply not only to the person who is entering active military service, but also to his or her dependents and those to whom the service person owes money. The protection begins when you receive orders to report for extended active duty and it ends a short period of time after separation from military service. This relief is not automatic. For example, when some form of legal action—like a lawsuit—affects your rights, *ordinarily* you must "trigger" the act by calling the court's attention to the fact that the Soldiers' and Sailors' Civil Relief Act may apply to you. (Your attorney can do this for you.) If the court decides that military service did *materially affect* your ability to comply, it will grant appropriate relief under the act.

CAN I GET MY CIVILIAN JOB BACK AFTER I'M OUT OF THE MILITARY?

Usually. If you join the military or are drafted, you have the right to be restored to your former position or one of similar status, seniority, and pay. You are also entitled to receive automatic pay increases which have been granted other employees during your absence. This law covers private, federal, state, county, and city employees.[4] To be eligible for your former position, you must meet the following requirements:

The employment was not temporary.

You left only because of your military service.

You did not serve more than four years active duty.

You are qualified to perform the duties of the position. If you were disabled in the service and cannot perform your former duties, you are entitled to receive the nearest comparable job with duties you can perform.

You must apply for restoration within ninety days after your release from active duty. If you are hospitalized, you have up to ninety days after your release from post-discharge hospitalization as long as you are not hospitalized more than one year.

IF I AM IN THE RESERVES OR NATIONAL GUARD, ARE THE PROVISIONS DIFFERENT?

No. You are entitled to the same job protection for part-time military service as well.

Chapter 432, Title 38, of the *United States Code* makes the following stipulations (with some specialized exceptions):

Your employer is required to excuse you from work for military training.

You cannot be discharged because you are in the reserve components or because you seek time off for military training.

You cannot be denied promotion because of your guard or reserve status.

Your employer cannot subtract your military training from your vacation time.

Your employer cannot limit the number of times you are required to perform military training.

As long as you are not absent for longer than four years (five years as a federal employee), you are entitled to your old job or its equivalent. 13

THE MILITARY CRIMINAL SYSTEM

The criminal laws of all branches of the military are contained in the Uniform Code of Military Justice (UCMJ), an act of law passed by the U.S. Congress and signed by the president.

The UCMJ prohibits "typical" crimes such as assault, theft, rape, and murder, but also covers distinctly military offenses: disobedience of an order, disrespect to an officer, and unauthorized absence (AWOL).

For the active-duty military member, the UCMJ applies at all times and in all places. Thus, spouse abuse occurring off-base and after normal duty hours may be punishable by the military.

Should you face trial by court martial for an offense arising under the UCMJ, you have the right to a military lawyer at no cost to you, regardless of your ability to pay for legal representation. Additionally, you have the right to your choice of military counsel, so long as he or she is reasonably available. Finally, you may hire a civilian attorney to represent you while also retaining your military attorney.

WHAT BENEFITS DO DEPENDENTS RECEIVE?

If you are on active duty, your husband and children can use military exchanges or commissaries (stores), theaters, clubs, and other facilities including the hospital and dental clinic. There are many regulations about medical care. Before you join, you should get detailed information about the medical benefits your family would be entitled to. This information is available at any military post or at CHAMPUS (Civilian Health and Medical Program of the Uniformed Services) in Denver, Colorado 80240. Also see Department of Defense Pamphlet Pa-3B, "Uniformed Services Health Benefits Program."

Generally, your husband and children under twenty-one are entitled to use medical facilities on a military post. If there is no space or facility available or if they are not living near a military installation, they are entitled to use a civilian facility at government expense under the CHAMPUS program. Not all facilities will accept dependents under this program. Also, there are some expenses that you must pay. Except in emergencies, you should obtain authorization from the military medical facility to use CHAMPUS.

CHAMPUS is a cost-sharing program designed to help you pay for authorized medical services obtained from civilian sources. It is important, when your dependents receive medical care from a civilian physician or hospital, to determine at the outset that the care giver will accept the CHAMPUS reimbursement as full payment for his or her charges. (CHAMPUS has a fee schedule for all types of services.) If the CHAMPUS payment is not accepted as full payment, your dependents must pay the difference between what the physician or hospital charges and the amount of the CHAMPUS reimbursement.

You should get detailed information about the health care benefits available to dependents before you need it. Another benefit to dependents is that they (and you) can get free legal advice and help from any military installation with a Legal Assistance Office. These offices are staffed by JAC (Judge Advocate General Corps) officers, uniformed attorneys who are licensed to practice in at least one jurisdiction. It is very useful to get an expert opinion on planned legal actions such as signing a contract. The legal assistance officer cannot represent your dependents on some types of legal problems, such as in-court representation on civilian criminal charges, lawsuits between private parties, or lawsuits you may want to file against the military or federal government. However, even there, she can help them in finding a civilian lawyer.

14

CRIMINAL LAW: WHAT TO DO IF YOU ARE ARRESTED

WHAT IF I AM ARRESTED?

An arrest can be made by citation or by transportation to jail. If you have verifiable contacts in the community and the offense is a minor one, an arrest will be made by citation. If you are arrested by citation you sign a ticket and promise to appear voluntarily no sooner than five days and no longer than fourteen days from the date the ticket is issued.

When you appear at the court you are arraigned before a judge. If you do not have sufficient contacts in the community or if the crime is serious, you will be transported to jail. Once there you may be "booked." Booking consists of entering the alleged crime in an official ledger and obtaining photographs and fingerprints of the suspect. If the jail is overcrowded, you may be released at this point on a No Bail Release (NBR). Otherwise, you are placed in a cell to await an arraignment (the first court appearance) before a judge.

WHAT DO I DO AFTER ARREST?

You have a right to make at least two phone calls to your family, friends, lawyer, or bail bondsman. If the police question you about the alleged crime while you are in jail, you should be given your constitutional rights to remain silent and to speak with a lawyer before you answer any questions relating to the case. These are called *Miranda* rights because they were established in a court case where the defendant's name was Miranda.[1] Voluntary or contemporaneous statements you make about the alleged crime do not fall within the protection of the Miranda case and may be used against you in court.

Once you have been arrested, you can be held in jail only for a short time while the legal formalities are carried out. As soon as possible you must be taken before a judge for arraignment. At the time of arraignment the judge reads the charges against you, sets the conditions for release, and appoints a public defender if you cannot otherwise afford an attorney. Anyone arrested or accused of a crime is entitled to a lawyer. If you cannot afford to hire an attorney *and* there is a likelihood that you may be required to go to jail, the federal, state, or local prosecuting entity provides an attorney. You may be required to pay some of the costs of counsel at the end of the case if the representation results in a plea or conviction of the charges.

HOW CAN I BE RELEASED?

The judge who presides at arraignment makes the determination about conditions that will be required prior to release from jail. Release until the trial might be conditioned upon any of the following:

Bail

Supervised release

Personal recognizance

Agreeing to abstain from drugs and/or alcohol.

If you are released on bail, an individual or bail bondsman posts money with the court to ensure that you will return for trial. "Supervised release" in Salt Lake County is handled through pretrial services. In other parts of the state it is handled through a local agency or a responsible third party. "Personal recognizance" means that you are released on your promise to reappear.

WHERE WILL THE ARRAIGNMENT OCCUR?

Arraignment takes place in the county where you are arrested. If the offense occurred in a different county, you are transported to that place for arraignment, since according to Utah law a trial is held in the county where the offense occurred. After the arraignment you are free to return to your home until the next scheduled court date.

HOW ARE CRIMES CLASSIFIED?

The classification of a crime is based on its seriousness and on whether or for what period of time jail can be imposed. The most serious crime is capital crime (punishable by death). Felonies, the next level of crime, are divided into the subcategories of first degree (five years to life and/or $10,000), second degree (one to fifteen years and/or $10,000), and third degree (zero to five years and/or $5,000). Misdemeanors are less serious and are divided as class A (zero to one year and/or $2,500), class B (zero to six months and/or $1,000), and class C (zero to ninety days and/or $500). Infractions are the least serious type of crime and have a maximum fine of $500 and no possibility of a jail sentence.[2]

HOW ARE CHARGES BROUGHT AGAINST ME?

Charges must be by information or indictment. An information is the formal charging document that states your name, the alleged crime and the classification of the crime. In Utah the judge can arraign you from the summary of the charges listed on a citation. However, before
14 the trial begins you should receive a copy of the formal document filed against you. If the crime is greater than a misdemeanor, the judge requires a formal information and probable cause statement, which summarizes the charges against you and the basis upon which you appear to be the responsible person. You can waive your right to have the formal information read at any of the proceedings. If you do not waive this right, the judge will read the formal document to you.

An indictment is a charging document issued by a grand jury. This method is seldom used in the State of Utah.

WHAT HAPPENS NEXT IF I AM ACCUSED OF COMMITTING A FELONY?

If you are charged with a felony, the next hearing in Salt Lake is a roll call hearing. At this hearing the defense evaluates the prosecution's case and decides whether to waive the preliminary hearing. If the hearing is waived, the judge sets a date to take a plea and set the case for disposition. The case is then bound over to the district court. If the preliminary hearing is not waived, a date for the preliminary hearing is set. At the preliminary hearing the circuit court judge hears evidence presented by the prosecution and determines whether there is probable cause to have you stand trial for the alleged offenses. Many defense attorneys use this hearing to test the strength of the state's witnesses. The state does not try the whole case at this point, but it must put on enough of the case to satisfy the judge that there is reason to believe that a crime was committed and that there is sufficient reason to believe you are the responsible person. If the judge finds the evidence sufficient, you are "bound over" to the district court. At the district court you are arraigned or asked to enter a plea to the charges. Your plea must be guilty, not guilty, or *nolo contendere* (no contest, in Utah). If you refuse to enter a plea, the court will enter a "not guilty" plea on your behalf. Once the plea is entered, the judge sets a pretrial conference date, then a trial date. All of this process is governed by the right to a speedy trial.[3]

At the trial the state must establish the defendant's guilt "beyond a reasonable doubt." The judge or jury then reaches a verdict. If the defendant is found guilty, he or she is sentenced in no less than two nor more than thirty days unless he or she waives that right.

WHAT IF I WANT TO PLEA BARGAIN?

"The disposition of criminal charges by agreement between the prosecutor and the accused, sometimes loosely called 'plea bargaining,' is an essential component of the administration of justice. Properly administered, it is to be encouraged."[4] There is no way all of the criminal cases charged could be tried before a judge or jury without creating a backlog so great that the system would cease to exist. Therefore, plea negotiations are allowed in the courts. The recommendations that the prosecutor might make to encourage a plea are reductions of charges, dismissal of counts for pleas to other counts, or simply recommendations on the length and/or type of sentence to be imposed. The judge is not required to follow the recommendations of the prosecutor or defense attorney; however, a plea negotiation can be placed on the record before a defendant enters a plea and the judge will/must indicate an unwillingness to follow plea negotiations involving dismissal of charges for a plea before the defendant is required to enter his or her plea.

Any guilty plea, whether a straight guilty plea or a plea of no contest, must meet two requirements. It must be voluntary and intelligent, and it must be supported by a factual basis developed on the record. A no-contest plea is the same as a guilty plea for the purposes of punishment. The advantage to the defendant of the no-contest plea is that, unlike a guilty plea, it cannot be used against a defendant as an admission of guilt in a subsequent criminal or civil case.

WHAT ARE MY RIGHTS TO APPEAL?

An appeal may be automatic or discretionary, depending on the level of the original trial court and the type of crime. In Utah all cases except capital cases are heard by the court of appeals. Capital cases are directly appealed to the supreme court. The supreme court will also certify appeal cases that have a significant effect. An appeal must be taken within thirty days of the entry of the sentence.

WHAT IF I AM THE VICTIM OF A CRIME?

Victims of crime should contact the police immediately and give any information they have about the responsible person. If the person is still at the scene, the officer may initiate charges with a misdemeanor citation. If the crime is too serious for a citation or if follow-up is necessary, a detective is assigned to the case. He or she obtains the necessary information and screens the case with the appropriate prosecuting agency.

MUST I GO TO COURT?

If you report a crime to the police and a suspect is caught, you may have to appear in court. (This is not necessary if he pleads guilty to the charge.) You do not need to hire your own lawyer. The case is filed in the name of the city where the offense occurred, or in the name of the State of Utah. The city or county attorney handles the case for the city or state. Technically, you are only a witness in the prosecution.

DO I NEED AN ATTORNEY?

You may want to talk to a private attorney about the possibility of bringing a civil suit against the defendant to obtain a money judgment against him for the damages and suffering he caused you. If you were assaulted on the premises of a "third party" (someone's property other than your own), you may want to ask an attorney if the property owner violated his or her duty to maintain safe premises. For example, there may have been insufficiently secure doors in a hotel or insufficient lighting in a store's parking plaza. You would be the plaintiff in any civil action filed and you would have more control over a civil lawsuit than you have as a witness in the criminal prosecution. There is nothing to prevent you from proceeding with both a criminal prosecution and a civil lawsuit at the same time.

WHAT ELSE SHOULD I KNOW?

There is a relatively hidden world that exists in criminal law. It is called "discretion." The police, the prosecutor, and the courts all have varying degrees of power to "push" a case or to drop it altogether, depending upon the stage the case has reached. Their decisions can have as much significance for the accused as any opinion delivered by the Supreme Court. A police officer can decide not to report a first offender (usually in a minor case such as speeding), a prosecutor can refuse to accept a plea, and a judge can divert a case out of the criminal system.

The criminal justice system is designed to serve justice and does not always right every wrong. Beware of the limitations of the system, but do not hesitate to use it if you are victimized.

CHART OF COURT PROCEEDINGS

FELONY *(punishable by death or imprisonment in prison)*	MISDEMEANOR *(punishable by imprisonment in local jail and/or a fine)*

ARRAIGNMENT

1. Be advised of constitutional rights.
2. Receive copy of complaint.
3. Enter plea of not guilty.
4. Appointment of counsel or request continuance to obtain own counsel.
5. Bail setting.

PRELIMINARY EXAMINATION

1. If complaint is filed, hearing is held to determine if probable cause exists to hold defendant to answer on the charges. (If grand jury indictment is filed, defendant may not be entitled to this hearing.)
2. Magistrate may dismiss case if evidence is insufficient.

Case may be settled prior to trial by plea bargain.

TRIAL

(Same general procedures as in misdemeanor cases)

SENTENCING

1. Court usually refers defendant to probation office for presentence report to include defendant's background, prior criminal record, and recommendation as to punishment.

ARRAIGNMENT

1. Be advised of constitutional rights.
2. Receive copy of complaint.
3. Enter plea of not guilty.
4. Appointment of counsel or request continuance to obtain own counsel.
5. Bail setting.

Case may be settled prior to trial by plea bargain.

TRIAL

1. Jury selection. (If court trial is conducted, jury waiver by defendant should be made.)
2. Opening argument by counsel.
3. Prosecution presents evidence such as clothing, documents, and demonstrative objects.
4. Defense presents evidence (or may elect not to present any evidence.)
5. Closing arguments by counsel.
6. Jury instructions given by judge.
7. Verdict is rendered (guilty/not guilty) or a mistrial is declared.

SENTENCING

(Same general procedures as in felony cases)

2. Sentencing hearing usually occurs within three to four weeks after conviction either by plea bargain or guilty verdict rendered at trial.

15
FINDING A LAWYER

WHAT SHOULD I DO IF I NEED A LAWYER AND DON'T KNOW ONE?

If you need to enforce or defend your legal rights, you can call or visit the Utah State Bar's Lawyer Referral Office at 645 South 200 East, Salt Lake City, UT 84111. The phone number is 531-9075.

When you have explained to the people in this office what your particular legal problem is, they will give you the names, addresses, and phone numbers of attorneys who work in that specific legal area. When you call an attorney for an appointment, be sure to tell him or her that you were referred by the Utah State Bar. The attorney is obligated to meet with you for an initial half-hour consultation for a fee of $15. You should be sure to discuss fees if it looks as though you will continue to work together, because the $15 limit applies only to the first visit.

WHAT SHOULD I KNOW ABOUT ATTORNEYS' FEES?

Do not hesitate to call a lawyer to inquire about the fee for consultation. You will not be charged for this initial phone conversation. Lawyers have a variety of fee arrangements available depending on the type of case and the client's financial circumstances. Whichever arrangement you and your lawyer agree upon, you should make sure that you have a clear understanding of what the fee will be and that you get a fee agreement in writing.

Some of the more common types of fee arrangements are the flat fee, the hourly rate, and the contingent fee.

The flat fee is a specific amount of money for which a lawyer agrees to perform specific legal services. For example, a lawyer may charge a flat fee of $300 for a simple, uncontested divorce, a flat fee of $600 to incorporate a small business, or a flat fee of $150 to draft a simple will. A flat fee arrangement usually implies that the lawyer will render the ''customary and necessary'' legal services that another lawyer in the same area would render in the same kind of case. It is very important that you and your lawyer have a clear agreement in writing as to what a flat fee does and does not cover.

Sometimes there is no way of knowing at the outset what a particular legal matter will involve. In cases where a lawyer cannot accurately estimate a total fee, an hourly rate is often the best arrangement. An hourly fee might also be desirable when a client wishes to have a lawyer do some preliminary research and give a legal opinion regarding a question or problem (for example, whether to bring a lawsuit). Because hourly fees charged by lawyers vary widely, it is important that you have a clear understanding of the fixed rate per hour before agreeing to this arrangement.

Contingent fee arrangements allow a client to pursue a lawsuit which might otherwise be impossible. They are often used in negligence, personal injury, and collection cases, to name a few. (They are illegal in divorce or criminal cases.) A lawyer who takes a case on a contingency basis usually does so because the client has limited financial resources and the lawyer feels that there is a good chance to win the case.

15

In a contingent fee arrangement, the lawyer takes a fee only if money is recovered. This fee will be an agreed-upon percentage of the amount recovered. If your case produces no money, your lawyer is not paid for time and services. You, the client, however, must bear all court costs and out-of-pocket expenses related to the case.

Lawyers' percentages in contingent fee arrangements are high, ranging from about one-third to as much as half. If you enter into such an arrangement, you should make certain the agreement is spelled out in writing. Be sure you understand what the percentage is, on what amount it will be calculated, and what costs and expenses you will be responsible for.

WHAT IF I CAN'T AFFORD A LAWYER?

Many services are still available. The American Civil Liberties Union specializes in problems based upon violations of civil liberties (such as your right to free speech) or discrimination (if you've been fired so they can hire a man, for instance). If your case falls within the ACLU's range of interests and would clarify the law in what it considers to be a needed area, it may assign an attorney to represent you without charge, no matter what your economic status or family income may be. The ACLU is located in the Boston Building, 9 Exchange Place, Suite 701, Salt Lake City, UT 84111. The phone number is 521-9289.

Another group offering legal services for a special kind of case is the Legal Center for People with Disabilities at 455 East 400 South, Suite 201, Salt Lake City, UT 84111. The phone number is 363-1347. This office provides legal services to people who are developmentally disabled, which means that they have a chronic mental or physical disability that was present before they reached the age of twenty-one and is likely to continue indefinitely. The center's fees are based on family income and range from no charge to around $15 for each consultation.

There are two groups that will help you with legal services of a more general nature. The Legal Aid Society, at 225 South 200 East, Suite 230, Salt Lake City, UT 84111 (328-8849), will provide legal assistance based on family income. You may call the Legal Aid Society for information regarding income guidelines, as each case is evaluated individually. This office serves only residents of Salt Lake County and specializes in problems involving domestic and family law: child custody, divorce, and similar matters.

The Legal Aid Society works closely with another agency, Utah Legal Services, Inc., at 245 South 400 East, Salt Lake City, UT 84115

(328-8891). The Legal Aid Society will refer to Utah Legal Services most of its cases involving income maintenance (i.e., welfare payments, Medicaid, aid to dependent children, Supplemental Security Income, etc.), landlord-tenant disputes, and immigration problems. Utah Legal Services will, in turn, refer most of its family law cases to the Legal Aid Society. However, Legal Aid operates only in Salt Lake County, while Utah Legal Services, Inc., has offices in Salt Lake, Provo, Ogden, and Cedar City. Utah Legal Services charges no fee, but provides services only to the poor. The National Legal Services Corporation sets income guidelines based on the family's gross monthly income and the number of people supported by that income.

WHAT CAN A LAWYER DO FOR ME?

Because you probably do not have an attorney's extensive knowledge of the law, you may not be aware of how much a lawyer can do to help in some circumstances. A lawyer can help keep you out of legal trouble, assure that your legal transactions are handled properly, or assist you if you should get into legal difficulty. Certain transactions should never be undertaken without a lawyer. Among these are adopting a child, buying or selling property, filing for bankruptcy, making or changing a will, starting a business, getting a divorce, facing a lawsuit against you, or suing someone else (unless in small claims court as described in chapter 16). It is unwise to assume that you do not need or cannot afford a lawyer. It is a much better policy to investigate the services mentioned in this chapter and determine whether and how a lawyer can help you.

Finally, if you would simply like to discuss a problem to ascertain whether further legal advice is needed, you can contact the Utah State Bar and make an appointment through the Tuesday night Bar-Ask-a-Lawyer program. As a public service, members of the Utah State Bar have volunteered to be at the Law and Justice Center located at 645 South 200 East on Tuesday evenings to listen to problems from members of the public. If further referrals are required, they can be made that night.

16

SMALL CLAIMS COURT: THE PEOPLE'S COURT

WHAT IS SMALL CLAIMS COURT?

Small claims court is where legal issues and problems that are based on contracts, service disputes, and other claims having a value less than $1,000 can be argued before a judge. A small claims hearing allows each side to state why money is or is not owed, and then a decision about the claim is made by the judge.

WHO USES THE COURT AND WHEN?

Any individual or business may use a small claims court if the problem can be settled for $1,000 or less. Examples of cases that are appropriate for filing in small claims court are—

A tenant sues a landlord for not returning a rent deposit when the apartment was left in the condition agreed upon in the original lease or contract.

A retail merchant sues a customer for failing to pay for an item that was purchased and used.

A customer sues a dry cleaner for refusing to replace an expensive garment ruined as a result of a poor or inappropriate cleaning method.

A driver of an automobile sues another driver for damage to his or her car that is not covered by insurance.

Although any one of these cases can be a real problem for you, it may not have a large enough monetary value to warrant hiring an attorney or paying for a full court hearing. The small claims court offers a way for individuals to solve these problems themselves in a faster and less expensive manner than a regular court proceeding.

WHEN IS COURT HELD?

Small claims court hearings are usually held in the evenings. Salt Lake Department cases are held in the circuit court located at 451 South 200 East, Salt Lake City, Utah 84111 on Tuesday, Wednesday, and Thursday.

WHO ACTS AS THE JUDGE?

Members of the Utah State Bar are sworn in to act as *pro tem* (temporary) judges. They have all the power of judges who sit in the daytime, but they are not paid. They voluntarily serve in the court to keep costs down and to aid citizens in resolving their problems. If they do not give a decision on the night of the court, they will issue a written decision later.

DO I NEED AN ATTORNEY?

You do not need to hire an attorney to sue in small claims court. In fact, in most cases attorneys are discouraged from attending.

HOW MUCH DOES IT COST AND HOW MUCH CAN I RECOVER?

The cost of small claims court is usually under $40, which includes payment of a filing fee and process server fee. The fee is well below the national average for the cost of filing a lawsuit in the circuit or district courts. You can sue for a maximum of $1,000. In addition to that amount you can recover the amount you spent to bring the defendant to court.

HOW DO I FILE AND PREPARE FOR COURT?

1. *Call the small claims court to see if the court can hear your case.*

Small claims courts can hear a case only if they have jurisdiction, or authority, over the claim and the person you are suing. If the problem occurred within the territorial limits of the court, the judge can hear the case. Small claims territory comprises the same area defined by other state courts. The court can also obtain jurisdiction over the case if the person you are suing lives within the territory of the court.

After determining that the court has jurisdiction over your claim, the clerk at the court will help you prepare the documents you need to file to start a court case. You must fill out an affidavit, sign it, and certify that what you have stated in it is true. The case is then filed with the court, and a copy must be delivered to a constable or sheriff who will serve the defendant and set a date for trial. In Salt Lake County, you can call the following numbers for assistance:

Salt Lake Department	533-3911
Murray Department	261-0562
Sandy Department	533-7887
West Valley Department	533-7890

2. *Observe a session of court before your trial date.*

All small claims actions are open to the public, so you can easily attend a case before your court date. This will show you what to expect and will make your night in court run more smoothly.

3. *Bring all papers and facts about your case to court.*

This information may include cancelled checks, purchase orders, written estimates, contracts, leases, or anything in writing that explains why you think you have been wronged by the other party. Organize your documents in chronological order and be sure to check them carefully. Accurate records can be very important to the outcome of the case.

4. *Bring expert/impartial witness.*

If your claim deals with the adequacy of a service or workmanship, or if the amount of damages can be determined by an expert (such as a police officer in an accident case), you will need to subpoena the disinterested party to be a witness in your case. Under the rules of evidence, you cannot tell the judge what a third party has told you. That party must be present in court to testify for you.

5. *Tell your story.*

When you go to court, the plaintiff (the person who filed the claim) speaks first. After the plaintiff tells his or her side of the story and presents documents, the defendant will be allowed to ask the plaintiff questions. The defendant then presents his or her case, after which the plaintiff can ask questions. The judge may also ask questions of any of the witnesses who are in the court and will usually give a decision on that night.

Don't worry that you don't know legal jargon. The court wants citizens to tell their own stories. Simply state your case, identify the problem, and tell the judge why you think you should receive monetary damages.

If you have a good case the facts will speak for you.

WHAT DO I DO ONCE I GET A JUDGMENT?

If you win, you will receive a judgment against the individual you sued. This obligates the individual or business to pay you the amount awarded to you by the judge. If an appeal is not taken within ten days, you can file post-judgment actions against the party. These will bring the defendants back to court to testify under oath when they will pay you. If you have any problems, call the clerks at the court and they will help you file the next order in the court.

NOTES

CHAPTER TWO. Employment

1. *DeSantis v. Pacific Telephone and Telegraph Co.* 608 F.2d 327 (9th Cir. 1979).

CHAPTER FOUR. Children: Child Care, Adoption, Support, Protection, Rights of Minors, and Education for the Handicapped

1. UCA /s78-30-4(3).
2. UCA /s78-30-1.
3. UCA /s78-30-8.
4. UCA /s78-30-14.
5. UCA /s62A-4-301.
6. UCA /s78-30-9.
7. UCA /s78-3a-48(5).
8. UCA /s78-30-14.
9. UCA /s78-45-4.1.
10. UCA /s78-45-7.2 through 78-45-7.18.
11. UCA /s78-3a-19.
12. UCA /s62A-4-503.

13. UCA /s62A-4-511.
14. UCA /s62A-4-503.
15. UCA /s62A-4-509.
16. UCA /s78-3a-20.
17. UCA /s62A-4-513.
18. UCA /s76-5-404.1.
19. UCA /s76-5-406.5.

CHAPTER FIVE. Housing and Landlord/Tenant Relationships

1. UCA /s57-22-4.
2. *Id.*
3. UCA /s57-22-5.
4. UCA /s57-22-6.

CHAPTER SIX. Property Rights and the Making of a Will

1. *Peterson v. Peterson,* 571 P.2d 1360, 1361 (Ut. 1977).
2. *Id.*
3. Utah Constitution, Art. XXII, /s2.
4. UCA /s30-2-1, 30-2-5.
5. UCA /s30-2-1.
6. UCA /s3-2-6.
7. UCA /s30-2-8.
8. UCA /s30-2-9.
9. UCA /s75-2-201 *et seq.* 207.
10. UCA /s75-2-201.
11. UCA /s75-2-201 *et seq.* 207.
12. UCA /s75-2-202.
13. UCA /s75-2-502.
14. UCA /s75-2-503.
15. UCA /s75-6-103, 106.
16. UCA /s75-6-101(14).
17. UCA /s75-6-104(3).
18. UCA /s75-2-102.
19. UCA /s75-2-104.
20. UCA /s75-2-107.
21. UCA /s75-2-108.
22. UCA /s75-2-112.
23. UCA /s75-2-109(a).
24. UCA /s75-2-109(b).
25. For a general discussion of the factors considered by the courts in determining the validity of antenuptial and

postnuptial agreements, see *Scherer v. Scherer* 249 Ga. 635, 292 S.E.2d 662 (1982), an antenuptial case. Utah's position appears to be that courts, while not bound to abide by postnuptial agreements between spouses in determining property settlements, should respect them and give them great weight. See *Mathie v. Mathie,* 12 Utah 2d 116, 363 P.2d 779 (1961); *Pearson v. Pearson,* 561 P.2d 1080 (Utah 1977); *Naylor v. Naylor,* 563 P.2d 184 (Utah 1977). Utah courts are likely to apply this same theory to antenuptial agreements.

CHAPTER SEVEN. Utah Marriage and Divorce Law

1. UCA /s30-1-2(4) & (5) (1953), as amended.
2. UCA /s30-1-2 (1953), as amended (also UCA /s30-1-9).
3. UCA /s30-3-1 (1953), as amended (also incl. UCA /s30-3-2).
4. UCA /s30-4-1 (1953), as amended (also incl. UCA /s30-4-3 and /s30-4-5.
5. *Id.*
6. UCA /s30-1-17 (1953), as amended.
7. UCA /s30-1-1 (1953), as amended.
8. UCA /s30-1-2 (1053), as amended.
9. UCA /s30-3-7 (1953), as amended.
10. UCA /s30-3-10 (1953), as amended.
11. *Kallas v. Kallas,* 614 P.2d 641, 645 (Utah 1980).

CHAPTER NINE. Social Welfare Laws

1. 42 USC /s/402-431.
2. 42 USC /s414; 20 CFR /s/s404.101-110.
3. 20 CFR /s404.410(a).
4. 42 USC /s402-w.
5. 20 CFR /s404.330(d).
6. 42 USC /s423-d-1-A and /s1382c-a-3-A.
7. *Weinberger v. Weisenfeld,* 420 U.S. 636 (1975). Formerly only women were entitled to these ''mother's benefits''; under this decision a father can now receive payments on the same basis widowed mothers have in the past.
8. See note 2.
9. 42 USC /s415(b); 20 CFR /s404.212.
10. 20 CFR /s404.130-b-c-d.
11. 20 CFR /s422.110.
12. 20 CFR /s404.330.

13. 20 CFR /s404.335.
14. 42 USC /s402-e.
15. 20 CFR /s404.332-b-6.
16. 20 CFR /s416.110.
17. 42 USC /s1381 *et seq.*; 20 CFR /s416.101-416.2119.
18. 42 USC /s/s1395 *et seq.*; 20 CFR.
19. Utah Department of Social Services Assistance Payments Administration Volume 11 (Financial Assistance) /s/s218-222.8; /s/s240-242; /s/s306-338; /s/s400-440.
20. Unemployment compensation, UCA /s35-4-1 *et seq.* (1953).
21. UCA /s35-4-3 (1953).
22. *Turner v. Dept. of Employment Security,* 423 U.S. 44 (1975).
23. Utah Worker's Compensation Act, UCA /s35-1-1 *et seq.* (1953).

CHAPTER TEN. Taxes

1. There are other filing status categories in addition to those described in this article. These are primarily for individuals who are sixty-five and over or who are blind.
2. Rev. Rul. 58-66, 1958-1 C.B. 60.
3. Even if you are not legally divorced, you may be able to file as head of household if you can establish that you are an "abandoned spouse." You can make such a showing if (a) you paid more than half the cost to keep up your home; (b) you lived apart from your husband for the last six months of the year; and (c) your household is the principal residence for more than half the year of a child or stepchild for whom you can claim a dependency exemption. (An abandoned spouse can also file as a single taxpayer. However, the rates for filing as head of household are more favorable.)
4. If you are a married person filing separately, you may not claim the standard deduction if your spouse itemizes deductions. Section 63 of the Internal Revenue Code of 1986 (IRC).
5. IRC /s6013(d)(3).
6. IRC /s6013(e).
7. Adjusted gross income is gross income reduced by certain specified deductions. The more significant of these deductions are expenses incurred in carrying on a trade or business (but not most employee expenses); losses from the sale of property; deductions attributable to rents and royalties; and contributions to individual retirement accounts (IRAs).
8. IRC /s213(a).

9. IRC /s165(h).
10. IRC /s67.
11. IRC /s151(b).
12. IRC /s151(b).
13. IRC /s152.
14. A child is considered to be a student if, during each of any five calendar months of the year, he or she is in full-time attendance at an educational institution or is taking a full-time course of institutional on-farm training. IRC 151(c)(4).
15. IRC /s152(e)(1).
16. IRC /s152(e)(2).
17. IRC /s152(a).
18. Children include your son, daughter, stepson, stepdaughter, adopted son, adopted daughter, and a foster child who is a member of your household.
19. IRC /s151(c)(2).
20. IRC /s152(b)(3).
21. Treas. Reg. 1.262-1(b) (1972).
22. IRC /s215.
23. Rev. Rul. 73-200, 1973-1 C.B. 140, superseding Rev. Rul. 67-339, 1967-2 C.B. 126.
24. Rev. Rul. 73-201, 1973-1 C.B. 140, clarified by Rev. Rul. 73-603, 1973-2 C.B. 76.
25. Rev. Rul. 73-603, 1973-2 C.B. 76.
26. Rev. Rul. 55-261, 1955-1 C.B. 307, modified by Rev. Rul. 68-212, 1968-1 C.B. 91.
27. IRC /s21.
28. IRC /s71.
29. IRC /s47(e), 453B(g), 1015(e), and 1041.
30. See, e.g., *United States v. Davis*, 307 U.S. 65 (1962).
31. Treas. Reg. 1.71(d).
32. Rev. Rul. 74-153, 1974-1 C.B. 20.
33. Rev. Rul. 59-5, 1959-1 C.B. 12.
34. IRC /s85.
35. IRC /s86.
36. IRC /s101.
37. IRC /s101.
38. Rev. Rul. 70-281, 1970-1 C.B. 16.
39. Rev. Rul. 55-330, 1955-1 C.B. 381-34.
40. Rev. Rul. 72-605, 1972-2 C.B. 35.
41. IRC /s2010, 2505.

CHAPTER ELEVEN. Money Problems and Bankruptcy

1. Title 11 of the United States Code as amended (USC). The code is effective for cases filed after 30 September 1979.
2. 11 USC /s101(9) (1978).
3. 11 USC /s101(4) (1978).
4. 11 USC /s362 (1978), as amended by P.L. 98-353 (1984).
5. 11 USC /s101(31), as amended by P.L. 98-353 (1984).
6. 11 USC /s101(41), as amended by P.L. 98-353 (1984).
7. 11 USC /s522 as amended by P.L. 98-353 (1984).
8. The Bankruptcy Code gives each state the authority to impose its scheme of exemptions upon a debtor in bankruptcy rather than giving the debtor a choice between state and federal plans. In its 1981 session, the Utah legislature exercised this authority. The Utah exemptions statute is found in UCA /s/s 78-23-1 to 78-23-15.
9. 11 USC /s302 (1978).
10. 11 USC /s1301 (1978), as amended by P.L. 98-353 (1984).
11. 11 USC /s727 (1978), as amended by P.L. 98-353 (1984).
12. 11 USC /s523 (1978), as amended by P.L. 98-353 (1984).
13. 11 USC /s523 (a) (2) (1978), as amended by P.L. 98-353 (1984).
14. 11 USC /s523 (a) (1) (1978), as amended by P.L. 98-353 (1984).
15. 11 USC /s524(a) (1978), as amended by P.L. 98-353 (1984).
16. 11 USC /s524(c) (1978), as amended by P.L. 98-353 (1984).
17. 11 USC /s1328 (1978), as amended by P.L. 98-353 (1984).
18. 11 USC /s727(a) (8) (1978).
19. 11 USC /s1328 (1978), as amended.
20. 11 USC /s727(a)(8) and (9) (1978), as amended.

CHAPTER THIRTEEN. Women and the Military

1. Army regulations available at any Army installation.
2. *Title X*, USC /s1072, 1076, 1086.
3. 50 App USC /s501 *et seq.*
4. Veterans Reemployment Act, 38 USC /s20-21.

CHAPTER FOURTEEN. Criminal Law

1. *Miranda v. Arizona*, 384 U.S. 436 (1966).
2. Utah Criminal Code /s76-3-101 - 76-3-201. Utah Code Ann.
3. *Klopfer v. North Carolina*, 386 U.S. 213 (1967).
4. *Santobello v. New York*, 404 U.S. 257, 260 (1971).

RESOURCES FOR FURTHER HELP

AMERICAN CIVIL LIBERTIES UNION (ACLU)
Boston Building, Suite 701
9 Exchange Place
Salt Lake City, Utah 84111-2709 Phone: 521-9289

HOURS: 9:00 a.m.–5:00 p.m.
PURPOSE: To defend the Bill of Rights through litigation, legislation, and public education. Litigation is limited to precedent-setting and class-action cases.
SERVICES: Assesses complaints for their potential of advancing goals and objectives of the organization and provides direct representation when these conditions are met. Makes referrals, when possible, for other types of problems.
FEES: None.

ORGANIZATION STATUS: Private, nonprofit.

BETTER BUSINESS BUREAU OF UTAH

1588 South Main Street
Salt Lake City, Utah 84115 Phone: 487-4656

385 24th Street
Ogden, Utah 84401 Phone: 399-4701

Provo, Utah Phone: 377-2611

HOURS: 8:30 a.m.–5:00 p.m. (9:30 a.m.–4:00 p.m. by telephone)
PURPOSE: To provide information concerning the business community locally and out-of-state. Assists with complaints concerning local businesses, mail orders, magazine subscriptions, etc.
SERVICES:
1. Advisory services.
2. Public information.
3. Mediation/arbitration of complaints.

FEES: None.
ORGANIZATION STATUS: Private, nonprofit.

CONSUMER CREDIT COUNSELING SERVICE OF UTAH, INC.

845 East 4800 South, Suite 200
Murray, Utah 84107 Phone: 266-0064

HOURS: 9:00 a.m.–5:30 p.m.
PURPOSE: To help over-indebted families with budgeting and money management.
SERVICES:
1. Budgeting and personal money management help.
2. Educating families on the wise use of credit.
3. Setting up a "composition of debt" plan for liquidating indebtedness.
4. Referring families to other agencies when necessary.

FEES: Variable, up to $10 per month.
ORGANIZATION STATUS: Private, nonprofit; Member NFCC.

R

FAMILY SUPPORT CENTERS

PURPOSE: Prevention and treatment of child abuse.
SERVICES:
1. 24-hour crisis resident services for children, up to age eight, who are abused or in danger of being abused.
2. Parenting skills classes.
3. Parenting counseling.

FEES: Sliding fee scale for counseling services.
ORGANIZATION STATUS: Private, nonprofit; Department of Social Services contract service provider.

CHILD & FAMILY SUPPORT CENTERS

Child & Family Support Center
380 West 1400 North
Logan, Utah 84321
752-8880

Family Support Center of Ogden, Inc.
622 - 23rd Street
Ogden, Utah 84401
393-3113

Family Support Center
1360 East 1450 South
Clearfield, Utah 84015
773-0712

Sugarhouse Family Support Center
2020 Lake Street
Salt Lake City, Utah 84105
487-7778

Midvale Family Support Center
75 West Center Street
Midvale, Utah 84047
255-6881

Utah Valley Family Support Center
358 West 400 North, No. 4
Provo, Utah 84601
374-9080

Uintah Basin Family Support Center
Rt. 3 Box 3337
Myton, Utah 84052
545-2301

Cedar City Family Support Center
2075 West 3000 North
Cedar City, Utah 84720
586-0791

R

INDUSTRIAL COMMISSION OF UTAH

160 East 300 South, Third Floor
Salt Lake City, Utah 84111 Phone: 530-6800

HOURS: 8:00 a.m.-5:00 p.m.

PURPOSE: To provide better working conditions, especially in matters of safety and labor relations, and compensation for workers injured in industry. To handle all forms of employment discrimination.

SERVICES:
1. Industrial Safety: OSHA consultation and OSHA Division (530-6901).
2. Labor Division for problems arising relative to workers under 18 (530-6800).
3. Wage Claim Division (530-6800).
4. Industrial Accidents Division for questions arising from on-the-job injuries (530-6800).
5. Anti-discrimination unit (530-6800).

FEES: None.

ORGANIZATION STATUS: Public.

LEGAL AID SOCIETY OF SALT LAKE

225 South 200 East, Suite 230
Salt Lake City, Utah 84111 Phone: 328-8849
355-HELP(4357) Spouse Abuse

HOURS: 8:30 a.m.-12:00 noon and 1:00 p.m.- 5:00 p.m. weekdays except Tuesdays; Tuesdays 8:30 a.m.-12:00 noon and 2:00 p.m.-5:00 p.m.

PURPOSE: To provide legal representation to low-income individuals who are experiencing civil, domestic, or immigration legal problems.

SERVICES:
1. Legal representation in domestic matters centered in Salt Lake County (divorce, custody, child support, post-divorce modifications).
2. Emergency legal representation for victims of domestic violence seeking protective orders regardless of financial status.
3. Immigration representation to family members related to American citizens or permanent residents.

FEES: None.

ORGANIZATION STATUS: Private, nonprofit.

LEGAL CENTER FOR PEOPLE WITH DISABILITIES

455 East 400 South, Suite 201
Salt Lake City, Utah 84111
Phone: 363-1347; Toll Free: 1-800-662-9080

HOURS: 8:30 a.m.–5:00 p.m.
PURPOSE: To protect and advocate for the rights of individuals with mental and/or physical handicaps.
SERVICES:
1. Legal advocacy for eligible clients in Utah on issues relating to their handicaps.
2. Information and referral.
3. Presentations on the rights of individuals with handicaps.

FEES: None. Donations accepted.
ORGANIZATION STATUS: Private, nonprofit.

LEGAL DEFENDER ASSOCIATION, SALT LAKE

424 East 500 South
Salt Lake City, Utah 84111 Phone: 532-5444

HOURS: 8:30 a.m.–5:00 p.m.
PURPOSE: To represent indigent individuals in criminal cases. Must be appointed by the courts.
SERVICES: Legal representation in courts of Salt Lake County.
FEES: Courts may assess a fee.
ORGANIZATION STATUS: Public.

LEGAL SERVICES, INC., UTAH

124 South 400 East, Fourth Floor
Salt Lake City, Utah 84115 Phone: 328-8891

HOURS: 8:00 a.m.–5:00 p.m.
PURPOSE: To provide legal services to low-income clients on civil legal matters.
SERVICES:
1. Senior law services (over age 59).
2. Landlord/tenant services.
3. Claims with public agencies.
4. Civil legal problems (will not handle criminal cases).

FEES: None. Donations accepted.
ORGANIZATION STATUS: Private, nonprofit.

R

SALT LAKE RAPE CRISIS CENTER

2035 South 1300 East
Salt Lake City, Utah 84105 Phone: 467-RAPE

HOURS: 8:00 a.m.–5:00 p.m. (24-hour crisis line)

PURPOSE: To help victims and families cope with the trauma of rape. To provide educational and preventive services to the community.

SERVICES: Direct Services:

1. 24-hour Crisis Line: Provides prompt crisis intervention services to both immediate and past sexual assault victims and their families. These services include crisis counseling, advocacy, and assisting with emergency situations.
2. 24-hour Mobile Team: 25 specially trained volunteers provide on-call hospital crisis intervention and advocacy services to victims who have reported the crime and are taken to the hospital by police. Victims receive crisis counseling, advocacy, and preparation for a medical exam through five local hospitals. Families also receive crisis services, information, and support from a male and female volunteer intervention team.
3. Second Team: This crisis counseling program to assist victims of crime is designated to supplement initial crisis services provided by the frontline team volunteers. The team functions to provide short-term crisis assistance to primary victims of sexual assault, short-term crisis counseling to secondary victims, crisis services and advocacy for special population victims including minorities, children, adolescents, and nonreporting victims.
4. Victim Support Groups: A weekly support group of victims helping other victims deal with problems resulting from the assault. Secondary problems (job/security problems, relocation) which may arise are also dealt with, and these groups accommodate adult and adolescent victims.

Preventive/Educational Services:

1. Speaker's Bureau: Offers adult education presentations dealing with causes, effects, and prevention of sexual assaults.
2. "I'm in Charge!": A preventive-education sexual abuse program for elementary-school children. This program is designed to teach children to respond when confronted with a sexual assault situation.
3. Post Certified Police Training Program: A certified program developed with the assistance of the Utah State Police, which teaches officers the special needs of the sexual assault victim.
4. Adolescent Prevention Program: A junior-high and high-school program dealing with sexual assault prevention. Topics include date rape, male rape, and gang rape.
5. Training Sessions: Informational sessions for the community and interested volunteers about sexual assault and how to deal with a victim, his or her family, and an offender.
6. Parent-Child Sexual Abuse Program: A preventive-educational child sexual assault program for parents. Topics include dynamics, indicators, and prevention of child sexual abuse, and communication with children about sexual abuse.

FEES: None.
ORGANIZATION STATUS: Private, nonprofit.

SOCIAL SERVICES, UTAH STATE DEPARTMENT

120 North 200 West
Salt Lake City, Utah 84145-0500 Phone: 538-4171

HOURS: 8:00 a.m.–5:00 p.m.
PURPOSE: The Department of Social Services is the largest department in state government. It includes six divisions (Division of Aging and Adult Services; Division of Substance Abuse; Division of Family Services; Division of Services to the Handicapped; Division of Mental Health, Division of Youth Corrections) and four offices (Office of Recovery Services; Office of Assistance Payments; Office of Community Operations, and Statewide Offices of Com-

R

munity Operations) It also includes two state institutions (Utah State Hospital, Utah State Training School). The Department of Social Services provides a variety of services through its thirteen offices of community operations throughout the state. The staff in these offices determine eligibility for state and federal programs, and provide services to clients by contract and direct services. Services available to clients in all districts include adoptions, aging and adult services, aid to families with dependent children, day care, energy assistance, emergency work programs, family and individual counseling, food stamps, foster care, homemaker, Medicaid, protective services to children and adults, self-sufficiency, services to the handicapped, and social service health plan case management. In some districts the office also provides direct services for mental health, alcohol and drugs, and services under the county medically indigent program. If you experience problems with services at the community level you may call a toll-free number for the Department of Social Services (Payments: 1-800-662-3722 or Services: 1-800-331-4341) and discuss the difficulty.

DISTRICT OFFICES:

District 1 (Cache, Rich, Box Elder)
1050 South 500 West
P.O. Box 1000, Brigham City, Utah
84302
Phone: 723-8591

Sub Offices:
95 West 1st South
Logan, Utah 84321
Phone: 752-2511
(DFS Services Only)
Phone: 753-3683
(APA Services Only)

Rich County Courthouse
P. O. Box 417
Randolph, Utah 84064
Phone: 793-2015

125 South 1st West
Tremonton, Utah 84337
Phone: 257-0123;
(No F.S. Apps.)

R

Municipal Building
Garden City, Utah 84028
Phone: 946-2901
Thurs. Only 8 - 12
(No F.S. Apps.)

24-Hour On-Call Number:
Logan, 752-2511; Brigham City, 723-8591

District 2A (Morgan, Weber)
2540 Washington Boulevard, P. O. Box 349
Ogden, Utah 84402
Phone: 626-3300

24-Hour On-Call Number:
Ogden, 399-1371

District 2B (Salt Lake Central District)
2835 South Main
P. O. Box 15729
Salt Lake City, Utah 84115
Phone: 468-5400

Sub Offices:
Downtown
158 South 200 West
P.O. Box 45490
Salt Lake City, Utah 84145
Phone: 524-9000

254 West 400 South
Salt Lake City, Utah 84101
Phone: 533-4184

HEAT Services ONLY
(Oct. 15 - Mar. 31)

ZIP CODES SERVED
84101, 84102, 84103, 84105, 84108, 84109, 84111, 84112, 84113, 84115, 84117

24-Hour On-Call Number:
487-9811

District 2C (Davis)
1350 East 1450 South
P. O. Box 825
Clearfield, Utah 84015
Phone: 776-6112

Sub Offices:
470 East Medical Drive
Bountiful, Utah 84010
Phone: 295-4665 and 295-9474

24-Hour On-Call Number:
Davis County, 544-1298

District 2K (Salt Lake Valley West District)
4115 West 5295 South
Kearns, Utah 84118
Phone: 964-7700 (DFS Services only)

Sub Offices:
4095 West 5295 South
Kearns, Utah 84118
Phone: 964-7700
(APA Services only)

Westside - 2R/2K2
55 North Redwood Road
Salt Lake City, Utah 84116
Phone: 533-4310

ZIP CODES SERVED

2K2	84016, 84044, 84118, 84119, 84120
2R	84104, 84116

24-Hour On-Call Number:
SL West, 487-9811;

District 2S (Salt Lake South Valley District)
7292 South State
Midvale, Utah 84047
Phone: 255-8475

Sub Office:
101 East 7200 South
Salt Lake City, Utah 84047
Phone: 566-4328
(HEAT Serv. Only)
(Oct. 15–Mar. 31)

ZIP CODES SERVED
84006, 84065, 84088, 84093, 84121, 84020, 84070, 84091, 84094, 84123, 84124, 84047, 84084, 84092, 84107

24-Hour On-Call Number:
SL South, 487-9811

District 2T (Tooele)
47 South Main, Room 300
Tooele, Utah 84074
Phone: 882-5550
355-1539 (SL Direct)

Sub Offices:
255 South 1st East
Tooele, Utah 84074
Phone: 882-3323 (MH Svcs.)

59 East Vine
Tooele, Utah 84074
Phone: 882-2870 (AGING)

Bonneville Heights Division
P. O. Box 1180
Wendover, Utah 84083
Phone: 665-2231(2)

24-Hour On-Call Number:
Tooele, 882-5600

District 3 (Utah, Wasatch, Summit)
150 East Center Street
Provo, Utah 84601
Phone: 374-7800

Sub Offices:
89 North 100 East
Heber, Utah 84032
Phone: 654-1541

1764 Prospector
P. O. Box 680247
Park City, Utah 84068
Phone: 649-6018

280 East Center St.
Kamas, Utah 84036
Phone: 783-4393
Tues. ONLY 9–12

County Courthouse
2nd Floor
Coalville, Utah 84017
Phone: 336-4451
Tues. ONLY 1–5

24-Hour On-Call Number:
Provo, 372-0461

R

District 4 (Juab, Piute, Millard, Sanpete, Sevier, Wayne)
201 East 5th North
P.O. Box 550
Richfield, Utah 84701
Phone: 896-8476

Sub Offices:
50 South Main, Suite 5
Manti, Utah 84642
Phone: 835-2861/835-6731

Main & Courthouse
P. O. Box 112
Nephi, Utah 84648
Phone: 623-1927

20 East 1st North
P. O. Box 589
Fillmore, Utah 84631
Phone: 743-6611 (DFS)
Phone: 743-5304 (APA)

252 West Main
Suite B-1
Delta, Utah 84624
Phone: 864-3869

Piute County Courthouse
Junction, Utah 84740
Phone: 577-2643; M–F 8–5

Wayne County Courthouse
Loa, Utah 84747
Phone: 836-2406; M–F 8–5

24-Hour On-Call Number:
Sevier, 896-6433; Juab, 623-1344;
Millard, 864-2755; Sanpete,
662-1526

District 5 (Beaver, Iron, Washington, Garfield, Kane)
168 North 100 East
St. George, Utah 84770
Phone: 673-9691

Sub Offices:
106 North 100 East
P. O. Box 309
Cedar City, Utah 84720
Phone: 586-3841

190 North 100 East
P. O. Box 72
Beaver, Utah 84713
Phone: 438-2443

115 West Center
Kanab, Utah 84741
Phone: 644-5885

565 North Main
P. O. Box 395
Panguitch, Utah 84759
Phone: 676-8866

405 South Main
Milford, Utah 84751
Phone: 387-2761
Wed. ONLY 8–5

(Services ONLY — NO F.S.
APPS.)

Tropic Scout House
Tropic, Utah 84776
Phone: 679-8713;
Tues. ONLY 12–5

(Services ONLY — NO F.S. APPS.)

90 North 100 West
Escalante, Utah 84726
Phone: 826-4317;
Fri. ONLY 10–3

(Services ONLY — NO F.S. APPS.)

Ticaboo School OR Ticaboo Ranger Station
Hanksville, Utah 84734
Phone: 684-2228 (SCHOOL)
Phone: 684-2212 (STATION)
As need basis, once a month

Services ONLY)
24-Hour On-Call Number:
St. George, 662-1778

District 6 (Duchesne, Daggett, Uintah)
1052 West Market Drive
Vernal, Utah 84078
Phone: 789-5850

Sub Offices:
855 East 2nd North (112-3)
Roosevelt, Utah 84066
Phone: 722-4594

(Mental Health) P.O. Box 570
c/o Professional Plaza
Duchesne, Utah 84021
Phone: 738-2494

24-Hour On-Call Number:
Uintah, Daggett, 789-5528;
Duchesne, 722-4474

District 7A (Carbon, Emery, Grand)
90 North 1st East
Price, Utah 84501
Phone: 637-6850

Sub Offices:
45 East 100 South
P. O. Box 697
Castle Dale, Utah 84513
Phone: 381-2387

267 North Main
Moab, Utah 84532
Phone: 259-6127 (APA)
Phone: 259-6128 (DFS)

24-Hour On-Call Number:
Carbon-Emery, 637-1621;
Grand, 259-8115 (This is the sheriff's office and they have a pager for the on-call worker.)

R

District 7B (San Juan)
522 North 100 East
Blanding, Utah 84511
Phone: 678-3211/E

Sub Offices:
San Juan County Courthouse
Monticello, Utah 84535
Phone: 587-2016

Montezuma Creek Clinic
Montezuma Creek, Utah 84534
Phone: 651-3294

Bluff Community Bldg
Bluff, Utah 84512
Phone: 672-2227;
Tues.-Wed.-Thur.
ONLY 9-3

San Juan, 587-2237 (This is the sheriff's office and they have a pager for the on-call worker.)

THE OFFICE OF RECOVERY SERVICES

Salt Lake Office
Administration/Operations
120 North 200 West
Salt Lake City, UT 84145-0500
(801) 538-4400

Ogden Office
2540 Washington Boulevard
Ogden, Utah 84401
(801) 626-3475

Provo Office
150 East Center Street, #2100
Provo, Utah 84601
(801) 374-7233

Richfield Office
201 East 500 North, No. 8
Richfield, Utah 84701
(801) 896-5461

Farmington Office
225 South 2nd West
P. O. Box 699
Farmington, Utah 84025
(801) 451-5087

St. George Office
168 North 100 East
St. George, Utah 84770
(801) 628-1732

FEES: Dependent upon economic status.
ORGANIZATIONAL STATUS: Public.

UTAH ISSUES INFORMATION PROGRAM

Room 10, 233 West 200 North
Salt Lake City, Utah 84103-1193 Phone: 521-2035

HOURS: 8:00 a.m.–5:00 p.m.
PURPOSE: An advocacy agency which represents low-income residents and agencies working to increase their representation in local, state, and federal decision-making processes.
SERVICES:
1. Advocacy on behalf of residents to help them achieve necessary services at the government levels.
2. Active engagement in state policy development in areas of social services, housing, employment, education, and taxation with government staff and elected officials.

FEES: None.
ORGANIZATION STATUS: Private, nonprofit.

UTAH STATE BAR

645 South 200 East
Salt Lake City, Utah 84111-3834 Phone: 531-9077

HOURS: 8:00 a.m.–5:00 p.m.
PURPOSE: Professional organization required of all lawyers practicing in the state. Supervised by the Bar Commission of Utah.
SERVICES: Provides a referral service for persons seeking legal advice.
FEES: Lawyer's dues.
ORGANIZATION STATUS: Private, nonprofit.

VICTIM COUNSELING PROGRAM

Salt Lake Valley Mental Health
231 East 400 South, Fourth Floor
Salt Lake City, Utah 84111 Phone: 363-7911

HOURS: 8:30 a.m.–5:00 p.m.
PURPOSE: To provide education and counseling to victims of crime and their families. The program helps victims and their families cope with the trauma and intimidation that are often caused by crimes such as rape, incest, sexual abuse, assault, and homicide.

SERVICES: 1. Short- and long-term counseling, including psychiatric evaluation, medication, educational classes, inpatient services, and 24-hour crisis assistance.
2. Education and criminal justice system information, including counselors who act as courtroom advocates for victim rights and well-being.
3. Coordination with community agencies and organizations to prevent and treat child sexual abuse.

FEES: Free of charge to victims and their families.
ORGANIZATION STATUS: Public.

YOUNG WOMEN'S CHRISTIAN ASSOCIATION OF SALT LAKE CITY (YWCA)
322 East 300 South
Salt Lake City, Utah 84111 Phone: 355-2804

HOURS: 24 hours.
PURPOSE: To promote a safe and healthy environment for women and children who are experiencing domestic violence. To provide education, information, and support that can assist women in making informed choices about their lives.
SERVICES: Services for battered women and their children; 24-hour crisis shelter; groups; individual casework; referral to free counseling and legal services; housing referral and assistance; day care; parent education; day camp; tutoring; art therapy; psychological assessment for children.
FEES: None.
ORGANIZATION STRUCTURE: Private, nonprofit.

Other Resource Listings

Excellent directories of various human service organizations throughout the State of Utah can be found in the Utah Senior Citizens' Handbook published by the Young Lawyers Section of the Utah State Bar, Needs of the Elderly Committee, and in Yellow Pages for the Family, compiled by the Governor's Conference on Strengthening the Family and distributed through the Department of Social Services and US West Direct.